PEOPLE OF THE DAY

by Peter Wynter Bee

Illustrated by Nick Higton

© People of the Day Limited, 2004
Sunnymede, New England Hill, West End, Woking, Surrey GU24 9PY
Tel: 01276 858037   Fax: 01276 859483
www.peopleoftheday.net

Text by: Peter F Wynter Bee
Illustrations by: Nick Higton
Cover design ideas by: Jessie Wynter Bee

A CIP catalogue record of this book is available from the British Library.

ISBN 0-9548110-0-3

Published by People of the Day Limited
Typeset by TWA Design

To my wife, Sarah, and children, Jessie and Bill, for their tolerance and encouragement.

The Gordon Foundation

Profits from the sale of this book are to go to The Gordon Foundation, the National Memorial to General Gordon who was killed at Khartoum in January 1885. The Foundation was established at the request of Her Majesty Queen Victoria.

The Gordon Foundation works to support Gordon's School, a non-selective voluntary aided school, currently aiming to raise £3.5 million to build a performing arts centre.

Major-General Charles George Gordon C.B.
'He was a man who devoted his life to the service of others, simple, heroic, a hater of iniquity, giving his heart to the young, the poor and the outcast, accepting the hardest of duties, but refusing wealth and honours. He counted his life as nothing if by any means he might lessen the miseries of mankind.'

Preface

As Chairman of The Gordon Foundation it is a great pleasure to be invited to write this Preface.

The Foundation's work is devoted to supporting Gordon's School, a non-selective voluntary aided state school, near Woking in Surrey and the National Memorial to General Charles Gordon.

Everyone involved with Gordon's School – Governors, Headmaster, Staff and Parents are hugely proud of everything that Gordon's represents. We especially value its unique ethos, its spiritual values, its academic achievements and its determination to excel in all that it does.

We need to keep our facilities up to date. To that end we are embarking on a major fund raising effort to build a modern Performing Arts Centre. We need £3.5m.

I want to thank Peter Wynter Bee, one of our Governors, for all that he has done in publishing this first edition of 'People of the Day'. This private initiative, brilliantly supported by Nick Higton's caricatures, has been a real labour of love. It is so generous of him to donate the profits to our fundraising effort.

Please buy lots of copies. Inscribe suitably and send them to your friends or place them in influential spots for others to enjoy and buy. If you are wondering why it is that you have not yet caught the 'Selector's' eye, please be patient. Your turn could come.

Sir Anthony Pigott
Chairman The Gordon Foundation

Contents

Foreword

Inspired by the likes of Spy and others drawing for Vanity Fair, at the end of the nineteenth century, I have, for many years, wanted to produce an annual of caricatures of famous people, with a short biography or profile on each of them. I very much hope this will be the first of a collection of such publications and that the individuals featured will recognise their own characteristics and positive achievements.

My initial interest in the caricatures of Vanity Fair was triggered, as a child, when I was in the attic at home. There I found seven framed Spy caricatures, collected by my grand father, and all signed by the individuals featured. From then on, like many others, I collected a number of the prints. I hope that all who collect these caricatures will derive the same enjoyment.

For this first volume I have chosen a fairly wide selection of characters from many walks of life and from many backgrounds, most will be familiar to the reader and at least some of the information about each may well be known. However, I trust that when reading the profiles a reaction of 'I didn't know that' will, on occasion, be heard.

The subjects range from the dyslexic entrepreneur to the chosen one of the Tibetan people and include the politically correct, and, the politically 'less' correct. They come from many backgrounds so their quotes vary tremendously, from the powerful president's French faux pas to the advice given on dealing with a cash crisis, a situation I fear too many may be familiar with.

I have chosen fifty individuals to be included in this first book plus one who can be identified as the joker. He is the joker, not because he has failed to achieve great things, but because he is likely to be less well known. Having said that,

however, I am sure on Mothering Sunday and Valentine's Day, the words Felton's Flowers will feature on the lips of many a City worker.

In the last hundred years the media, printing and the transmission of information have been revolutionised and therefore we are all inundated with information about famous people. Frequently we see caricatures, cartoons and photographs of them all. One thing that has not changed is the debate over the difference between cartoon and caricature. The dictionary defines a cartoon as 'a drawing executed in an exaggerated style for humorous or satirical effect', and it defines a caricature 'as a depiction of a person in which their distinguishing characteristics are exaggerated for comic or grotesque effect'.

Tommy Bowles founded Vanity Fair in 1868, and The Daily News in the autumn of 1869 asserted that the caricatures in Vanity Fair were not really caricatures. Bowles responded, first observing, that The Daily News was mistaken in its understanding of the meaning of caricature and he went on to say;

"The Daily News says that the 'original' and 'genuine' purpose' of caricature is that of 'giving amusement' by a droll presentation of persons and things, and laments the absence of the 'comic' element and the tendency to 'phantasmagoric extravagance' (whatever that may be) 'grimness' and 'grotesqueness', which it says characterise modern caricatures.

"I might very well altogether deny that these remarks apply to the cartoons of Vanity Fair, and say that there is not in any one of those caricatures which have been published with it either an essential feature of grimness, of grotesqueness, or an essential absence of comicality. There are grim faces made more grim, grotesque figures made more grotesque, and

dull people made duller by the genius of our talented collaborator 'Ape'; but their is nothing that has been treated with a set purpose to make it something that it was not already originally in a lesser degree"

He went on to say that the original and genuine purpose of caricature was not to invent a line or colour but 'to charge and exaggerate'. He felt that caricaturing was to make the bland more bland, the mild, milder, the persuasive, more persuasive; it was not to turn a person into someone else or invest him with qualities he did not possess, nor was it the function of caricaturing to overemphasis the obvious.

Bowles was assiduous in his use of the word caricature and not cartoon. The purpose of caricature was not to invent something new but to exaggerate what was already in existence. I have attempted to follow Bowles's use of the word caricature.

I am sure there will be debate and criticism over who has been included and who has been left out, but the attention is now on whom to include in the next volume. Perhaps, the famous, not those who have been famous for just fifteen minutes but those who have been regularly in the papers and on television over the last year and who have impacted on the lives of others to a greater extent than "the man on the Clapham omnibus". What is it that makes people famous? For an entrepreneur, it is because they never give up and always go the extra mile, leaving no stone unturned and treating every setback as an opportunity. For others, perhaps, it is their sheer ambition, determination and never being prepared to take no for an answer, together with the confidence in themselves that they can achieve their aims.

Having wanted to produce this book for some considerable time but having failed to find an artist to draw the caricatures, I was extremely lucky to contact an employment agency when looking for some temporary help in the office. Nick Higton was despatched as that temp and when he was not flat out working for us he spent his moments sketching. This was too good an opportunity to miss and I therefore explained my vision, set the challenge, to which he rose.

So, I would like to thank Nick for his dogged determination to produce this volume's caricatures, all of which have been done in his spare time. Together we both hope that this book will act as a catalyst to encourage other artists, perhaps as yet undiscovered, to participate in future volumes. If you are one of those artists then please do contact us.

HM The Queen
'Dedicated Head of State'

Following the abdication of her Uncle, Edward VIII, in 1935, she became Heir Presumptive to the throne of the United Kingdom. Born on 21 April 1926, the first child of the then Duke and Duchess of York, who subsequently became King George VI and Queen Elizabeth, she was brought up to serve her country with commitment and devotion.

Whilst she was educated at home, she did, at the age of eleven enrol as a Girl Guide and later became a Sea Ranger. Growing up in line to the throne she gradually entered public life making her first broadcast in 1940, at the age of 14, sending a message to all the children of Britain and the Commonwealth, particularly those being evacuated because of World War II. Later in the war she served in the ATS as a driver and mechanic.

Her first solo public engagement took place in April 1943 when she spent the day, as the newly appointed Colonel-in-Chief of the Grenadier Guards, with one of its tank battalions in Southern Command. Thereafter her public duties increased considerably leading to her first official overseas visit, which took place in 1947, when she went with her parents and sister on a tour of South Africa. During that tour she gave a broadcast in which she dedicated herself to the service of the Commonwealth.

Following her return from South Africa, her engagement to Philip Mountbatten was announced. He is the son of Prince Andrew of Greece and, like herself, a great-great grandchild of Queen Victoria. They were married in Westminster Abbey on 20 November 1947, and have four children and seven grandchildren. In 1997 they celebrated their Golden Wedding Anniversary.

In 1952, King George VI's illness forced him to abandon his planned visit to Australia and New Zealand. Instead, Princess Elizabeth, as she then was, went together with Prince Philip. On 6 February, during the first stage of this journey, whilst in Kenya, she received the news of her father's death and her accession to the throne. She was crowned in Westminster Abbey on 2 June 1953.

That winter she and Prince Philip finished the tour they had started and visited Bermuda, Jamaica, Fiji, Tonga, New Zealand, Australia, Ceylon, Uganda, Malta and Gibraltar. Since that time she has undertaken numerous tours of both the countries of the Commonwealth and non-Commonwealth. She has also travelled throughout Britain attending hundreds of official functions every year and meeting people from all walks of life. She is well briefed and thus able to speak to all she encounters with knowledge, interest and understanding.

As Head of State she is the head of the Navy, Army and Air Force of Great Britain and hosts other Heads of State when visiting Britain. She also maintains close contact with the Prime Minister with whom she generally has a weekly audience. She receives all Cabinet papers and a daily summary of events in Parliament.

Her Golden Jubilee was celebrated in 2002 marking 50 years since her Accession. Only five previous British monarchs have reigned for this period: Henry III, Edward III, James I, George III and Queen Victoria. During the Jubilee year she once again visited Australia, New Zealand, Jamaica and Canada.

She has a great interest, as did her mother, in horse racing and has bred and raced horses for many years, often visiting race meetings to watch her horses run.

HRH The Earl of Wessex KCVO
'Supporter of the Performing Arts and Youth'

The fourth child of the Queen and Duke of Edinburgh, he was born on 10 March 1964 and was christened Edward Antony Richard Louis. Until his marriage to Miss Sophie Rhys-Jones he was known as Prince Edward. However, at that time he was created The Earl of Wessex and Viscount Severn. It was also announced that he would eventually succeed to the title of Duke of Edinburgh.

He was initially educated by a private governess but, at the age of 7, went on to Gibbs pre-prep school in Kensington. He subsequently went to Heatherdown prep school, in Ascot, and then followed in his father's and brothers' footsteps, by attending Gordonstoun, in Scotland. After school he took a Gap year, part of which was spent as a House Tutor and teaching English and History at Wanganui Collegiate School in New Zealand.

In September 1983 he went up to Jesus College, Cambridge, where he studied History, graduating with a BA in 1986 and obtaining his Masters in 1990. In 1986 he achieved Gold in the Duke of Edinburgh's Award and since that time he has been closely involved with the work of the Awards as Trustee of the UK and the International Award and Chairman of the International Council of the IA Association. He is also a United Kingdom and International Trustee of the Scheme and wrote and narrated two films about the Scheme shown on BBC television in 1987.

In 1983 he joined the Royal Marines as a Second Lieutenant on their University Entry Scheme but left in 1987. His involvement with the armed forces recommenced with his appointment, in 2003, as Colonel-in-Chief of the Royal Wessex Yeomanry.

In 1987 he went into theatre production joining the Theatre Division of Lord Lloyd Webber's Really Useful Theatre Company. In 1993 he formed his own independent television company, Ardent Productions Limited. It produced a number of programmes including: thirty half-hour programmes on 'Crown and Country', the 'Cater Street Hangman' and a programme on the restoration of Windsor Castle after the fire.

In early 2002 he stopped active involvement with Ardent Productions Limited and took on more royal duties in support of The Queen.

He has always been a keen sportsman and whilst, due to injury, he had to give up rugby, he continues his interest in riding, sailing, skiing, badminton and real tennis. His great interest in sports, the theatre and opportunities for the young are reflected in the numerous organisations of which he is Patron or President.

The Countess also has taken on the patronage of many organisations and in July 2003 was appointed Colonel-in-Chief of Queen Alexandra's Royal Army Nursing Corps, a role formerly undertaken by Princess Margaret.

His marriage to Miss Rhys-Jones, who was born in Oxford on 20 January 1965, took place on 19 June 1999 in St George's Chapel, Windsor, near their home at Bagshot Park, Surrey. On 8 November 2003 the Countess gave birth to their first child, a daughter, named the Lady Louise Windsor.

Nic

The Rt Hon Tony Blair PC MP
'He made Labour electable'

Born, Anthony Charles Lynton Blair, in Edinburgh on 6 May 1953, the son of a barrister. After a short spell in Australia, he spent his early years in Durham, where his Father was a law lecturer but at the age of 14 he returned to Edinburgh to complete his schooling at Fettes College. From there he went on to study law at St John's College, Oxford. Whilst at Oxford he was the lead singer and guitarist in a rock group called 'Ugly Rumours'.

On graduation he worked briefly in Paris as a bar tender and insurance clerk before going to London to follow his father by becoming a barrister; he specialised in industrial and trade union law. He joined the Labour Party in 1975 and was called to the Bar in 1976. During his pupilage he met his future wife, Cherie Booth QC, whom he married in 1980, and they have four children; three sons and a daughter. Their youngest son, Leo, was the first child to be born to a serving Prime Minister in over 150 years.

He first stood as a prospective Labour Candidate in May 1982 at the by-election in the safe Conservative seat of Beaconsfield where he came third with approximately 10% of the vote.

In 1983, he won a seat in Parliament in the newly created constituency of Sedgefield, near his home town of Durham. In 1987 he became the Labour spokesman on Trade and Industry before becoming, in 1988, the Shadow Secretary of State for Energy. From 1989 to 1992 he had the employment brief and after the 1992 election Labour's new leader, John Smith, promoted him to Shadow Home Secretary and member of the National Executive Committee of the Labour Party.

In 1994, at 41, following the sudden and unexpected death of John Smith, he became Labour's youngest ever leader. He set out to modernise the Labour Party, to bring it back from the militant tendency towards the centre of British Politics. He convinced the Party to eliminate its antiquated Clause 4 in the Party's constitution, which aimed at a communist-inspired system of production, distribution and ownership, replacing it with a more modern statement of objectives. His approach earned him the nickname of 'The Moderniser' and he coined the phrase 'New Labour' to re-brand the reformed and modernised party.

In 1997 he brought the Labour Party to a landslide victory with a very large majority in the House of Commons thus giving him a clear mandate to carry out the reforms he wished to pursue, including changes to the House of Lords and the establishment of a Mayor of London.

His greatest achievement has been to transform the Labour Party into a party that was once again electable. Since coming to power he has carried out many radical constitutional reforms, worked very closely with the US in waging war on Iraq, successfully ridding that country of its dictator, but to date failing to bring peace to the country. His period in office has also seen reduced unemployment, but perhaps this has been achieved by the immense increase in bureaucracy and the number of state employees, funded by substantial tax increases and the decimation of pensions.

President George Bush
'43rd President of the United States of America'

Born on 6 July 1946 in New Haven, Connecticut, he grew up in Midland, Texas. Following in his father's footsteps he attended the prestigious Philips Andover Academy in Massachusetts before going on to obtain a degree from Yale in 1968. On matriculation he returned to Texas to join the Texas Air National Guard, learning to fly fighter jets, but avoided Vietnam.

The early 1970s have been described as his 'nomadic period' when he moved back to East Texas and worked, intermittently, as a management trainee and on US Senate campaigns in Florida and Alabama. In 1972 he went to Harvard Business School leaving with an MBA three years later. At that time he formed an oil and gas exploration company, Arbusto, which he later merged with Spectrum 7. As chairman of the merged group, he sold it to Harken Energy, in 1986, realising a considerable personal profit.

He then turned his attentions to supporting his father who had decided to run for President and although he had no official title he was a very trusted confidant to him. Shortly after his father's successful election in 1988 he formed a syndicate to acquire the Texas Rangers, a professional baseball team. He was the team's managing partner and became a well known figure. This clearly helped him to achieve his election as Governor of Texas in 1994.

His friendly nature, his appeal across party lines and minority voters, led to the Republican Party's realisation that he had the potential to run for President. In June 1999 he officially announced his intention to run for President and in July 2000 he announced his choice of running mate, Dick Cheney. In August that year they were formally nominated as the Republican candidates.

The battle for the White House against Gore and Lieberman was one of the closest and most disputed presidential elections in the country's history. Election night, 7 November 2000 saw confusion over whether or not he had won. It all hung on the state of Florida and its 25 electoral votes. After complicated legal battles he was eventually inaugurated as the 43rd President on 20 January 2001.

He will always be remembered for some of his great quotes, for example; "the problem with the French, is that they have no word for entrepreneur", but he will also be remembered for finishing the job his father had started a decade before of removing Saddam Hussein from Iraq. Sadly he has had considerable difficulty in securing the peace.

His time in office has been dominated by the aftermath of 11 September 2001, which led to his declaration of war on terror. In 2002, the UN resumed weapons inspections in Iraq, warning of "serious consequences" if Saddam Hussein failed to offer inspectors unrestricted access. Almost immediately after the UN resolution was passed, diplomats disagreed on whether the use of force was justified if Iraq did not comply. After months of debate and disagreement the US, in March 2003, declared war on Iraq without the support of the UN Security Council. It took four weeks to capture Baghdad and at that time President Bush declared that the major combat in Iraq was over. In December 2003 the US forces captured Hussein and Bush then announced, "a dark and painful era was now over".

In 1977, he married Laura Welch, a former teacher and librarian and they have twin daughters, Barbara and Jenna, known as Gin and Tonic to their security minders.

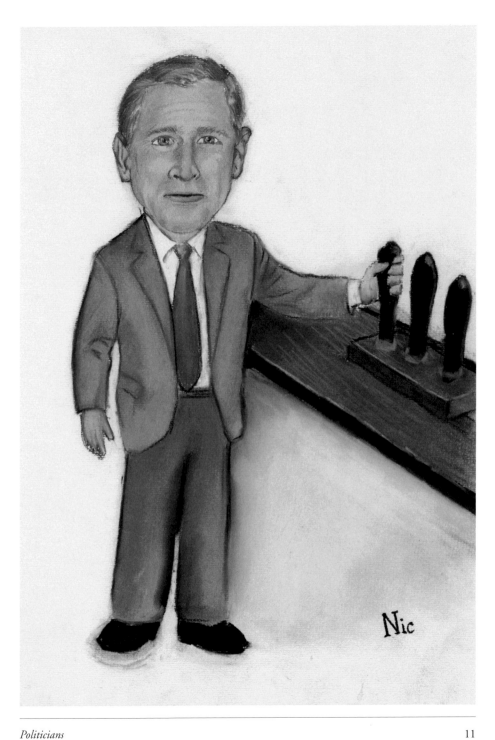

Senator Hillary Diane Rodham Clinton
'New York Senator'

She was born on 26th October 1947 in Park Ridge, Illinois. The daughter of a successful fabric store owner, Hugh Rodham, and his wife, Dorothy. She was their first child and was followed by two brothers Hugh and Tony. She went to school locally before going on to Wellesley College, from where she graduated in 1969. She went on from there to Yale Law School, graduating in 1973.

Following graduation she worked advising the Children's Defence Fund and also joined the impeachment inquiry staff, advising the Judicial Committee of the House of Representatives. She subsequently moved to Arkansas. There, in 1975, she married Bill Clinton, a fellow Yale Law School graduate, whom she met when she strode up to him in the library at Yale, with the words, "if you're going to keep staring at me, I might as well introduce myself".

She joined the faculty of the University of Arkansas Law School in 1975 and the Rose Law Firm in 1976, while her husband became Attorney General and then, in 1978, Governor of Arkansas. She served as Arkansas's First Lady for twelve years and chaired the Arkansas Educational Standards Committee, co-founded the Arkansas Advocates for Children and Families, and served on the Boards of the Arkansas Children's Hospital, Legal Services and the Children's Defence Fund.

In 1991, before many Americans had heard of her, she was named by The National Law Journal as one of the 100 most powerful lawyers in America.

She became a powerful, dynamic and valued partner to her husband, Bill, during his 1992 presidential campaign and following his election he named her to head The Task Force on National Health Reform. Inevitably there were criticisms of the decision and claims of nepotism, feminism etcetera.

Her eight year period as First Lady was not without its difficulties, including the attempted impeachment of her husband, in 1998. However, throughout his presidency and all his difficulties, she has resolutely stood by him. Following the end of her husband's term of office there was much speculation as to whether she would wish to remain in politics. In the summer of 1999 she formed an exploratory committee to prepare for a possible Senate bid to represent New York.

On 7th November 2000 she was elected United States Senator for New York, the first First Lady ever elected to the United States Senate. She was sworn in at the opening of the 107th Congress on 3rd January 2001. Following the terrorist attacks on the United States on 11th September 2001 she worked to secure substantial funding for the clean up and reconstruction of both the area and those affected by the tragedy.

She is married to former President Bill Clinton and they have one daughter, Chelsea, born in 1980, who graduated from Stanford University in 2001. Her first memoirs, Living History, were published in 2003.

Nelson Rolihlahla Mandela
'The struggle is my life'

He was born at Qunu, near Umtata in the Transkei, on 18th July 1918. His father, Henry Mgadla Mandela, was chief councillor to Thembuland's acting paramount chief. Following the early death of his father, in 1927, he became the Chief's ward and was groomed for the Chieftainship. However he set his heart on becoming a lawyer and contributing to the struggle for freedom of his people.

He was educated initially at a local mission school prior to going to Healdtown Methodist Boarding School. He then moved on to university at Fort Hare from which he was expelled following his participation in a student strike, in 1940, along with Oliver Tambo. He completed his degree by correspondence, obtained articles and then enrolled for his LLB at the University of Witwatersrand.

In 1942 he joined the African National Congress (ANC) and in 1944 he helped found the ANC Youth League, with the aim of organising mass support for the ANC and making it more of an activist organisation.

In 1948 the National Party came to power in South Africa with a mandate supporting increased racial discrimination, in response the ANC Youth League called for mass strikes, boycotts, protests and passive resistance.

In July 1952 he is arrested and charged for violating the Suppression of Communism Act, found guilty and given a suspended sentence. In December of the same year he opened, together with Oliver Tambo, the first black law firm in South Africa.

In 1956 he is arrested along with 150 others and tried for high treason. Much of his next five years is devoted to the 'Treason Trial' and in 1961 they are all found not guilty. However the 'armed struggle' is launched which causes him to go underground and then leave the country. On his return, in 1962, he is arrested, convicted and sentenced to five years. He is held on Robben Island.

Whilst serving this sentence he is charged with sabotage and attempting to violently overthrow the government. This trial was known as the 'Rivonia Trial' and he was given a life sentence and sent back on Robben Island.

During the 1980's PW Botha's offers of freedom on condition he renounced violence were robustly rejected but shortly after his release from imprisonment, by President de Klerk, on Sunday 11 February 1990, he and his compatriots agreed the suspension of the armed struggle, known as the 'Pretoria Minute'.

In 1991 the ANC, for the first time, held its annual conference in South Africa, at which Mandela was elected ANC president. Negotiations began between the government of President de Klerk and the ANC, which resulted in democratic elections for all races occurring in 1994 with Mandela being elected President.

In 1944 he married Evelyn Mase, a nursing student, living in Johannesburg. A year later they had a son Thembi but he sadly was killed in a car crash in 1969. They had a daughter Makaziwe, who died at 9 months but then they had a son, Makgatho and a daughter Maki. In 1957 they divorced and a year later he married Winnie Madikizela with whom he has two daughters, Zeni and Zindzi. He separated from Winnie in 1992 and they were divorced in 1996. He subsequently married Graca Machel, the widow of a former president of Mozambique.

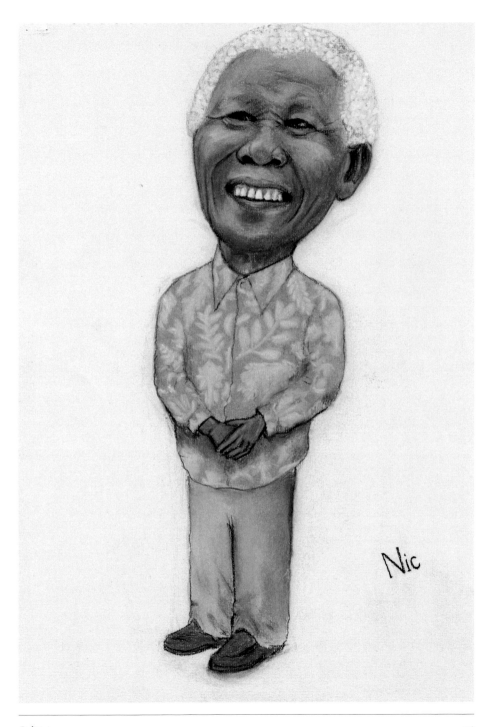

Kofi Annan
'Peacemaker'

He is the Seventh Secretary General of the United Nations and represents the well known face of the UN throughout the world. Born in Kumasi, Ghana, on 8 April 1938, to Henry and Victoria, a prominent family, where his father was an hereditary paramount chief of the Fante people. He studied at the University of Science and Technology in his birthplace before studying economics at Macalester College, in St Paul, USA. Continuing in economics, in 1961 he started a year's graduate studies in Geneva, prior to joining the World Health Organisation, based there, as an administrative budget officer.

He subsequently served with the UN Economic Commission for Africa, working in Addis Ababa; the United Nations Emergency Force, in Ismailia and the Office of the United Nations High Commissioner for Refugees, back in Geneva. He then moved to the UN Headquarters in New York, as Assistant Secretary-General for Human Resources Management and Security Coordinator for the UN System and then as Assistant General-Secretary for Programme Planning, Budget and Finance.

In 1990, following the invasion of Kuwait by Iraq, he was employed on a special assignment to facilitate the repatriation of more than 900 international staff and citizens from Iraq, subsequently leading the first UN team to negotiate with Iraq on the sale of oil in exchange for humanitarian aid.

Before being appointed Secretary-General, on 1 January 1997, he served as Assistant Secretary-General for Peacekeeping Operations and then as Under-Secretary-General. In the latter role he served as Special Representative of the Secretary-General to the former Yugoslavia, overseeing the transition in Bosnia and Herzegovina from the UN Protection Force to the multinational Implementation Force led by NATO.

As Secretary-General his first major initiative was his plan for much needed reform, "Renewing the United Nations", which was presented to the Member States in July 1997 and has been followed ever since. Inevitably in his position he becomes involved in many of the world's political problems, which have ranged from attempting, in 1998, to gain Iraq's compliance with the Security Council resolutions, on the one hand, to working to encourage the Israeli and Palestinian people to resolve their differences through peaceful negotiations based on Security Council resolutions 242 and 338 and the principle of "land for peace".

In April 2000, he issued a Millennium Report, entitled "We the Peoples: The Role of the United Nations in the 21st Century", calling on Member States to commit themselves to an action plan for ending poverty and inequality, improving education, reducing HIV/AIDS, safeguarding the environment and protecting peoples from deadly conflict and violence.

For his work with the UN and his continuing peacemaking efforts, he and the United Nations were together awarded the Nobel Peace Prize in 2001. He was appointed to serve a second term as Secretary-General, the term expiring on 31 December 2006.

His first marriage, to a Nigerian, with whom he had two children, a daughter, Ama and a son, Kojo, ended in divorce. However in 1984 he married Nane Lagergren, a Swedish lawyer and judge who has a daughter from her previous marriage.

Nic

President Putin
'Russian President'

Vladimir Vladimirovich Putin was born on 7 October 1952, in St Petersburg, formerly known as Leningrad, to Vladimir and Maria, the only child of his parents following the early death of his two brothers. His father was a factory foreman. Although officially prohibited in Communist Russia he was baptized into the Russian Orthodox Church.

As a boy he studied the martial arts and by 16 had become an expert at Sambo (a Russian style of self defence). He was selected to attend Leningrad School No.281, a school for the city's best students and in 1970 went on to Leningrad State University from which he graduated with honours, in 1975 having majored in civil law.

On graduation he was recruited into the KGB where he studied espionage and foreign intelligence based in Moscow, whilst there he learned German. He began working in counterintelligence prior to joining the KGB's First Directorate as a foreign intelligence agent.

In 1985, the KGB sent him to East Germany, to live in Dresden under a false name, with cover as the head of 'The German-Soviet Friendship Society'. His actual work included spying on member nations of NATO, recruiting informers and agents, and collecting and analysing data to send to Moscow.

With the rise of Mikhail Gorbachev and the collapse of Communism in Eastern Europe during the late 1980s, Putin's work in East Germany was quickly brought to an end. With the fall of the Berlin Wall and the reunification of Germany, Putin returned to Russia in 1990 and was given an administrative post at Leningrad State University, again largely as a cover for his continuing intelligence work.

He became interested in politics and left the KGB to support Anatoly Sobchak, his former law professor, who had become chairman of the city council and one of Russia's leading democrats. Sobchak was elected the first mayor of the newly renamed St Peterburg in 1991 and appointed Putin as his deputy mayor. He oversaw the daily administration of the City and was primarily responsible for the considerable foreign investment. Following Sobchak's failure to be re-elected in 1996, Putin resigned and was offered a Kremlin post as deputy to the head of the Kremlin Property department in Moscow.

In July 1998 he was appointed head of the federal security service, the main successor organisation to the KGB. During this period he was noted for his personal commitment and loyalty to President Yeltsin. President Yeltsin subsequently appointed him to be head of the security council.

In August 1999, Yeltsin named Putin as prime-minister and on 31 December 1999, Yeltsin resigned as President and appointed him to be acting President. Following his tough line on domestic and international politics and his hard-line stance against the Chechen rebels he became Russia's most popular politician and was elected president in the first round on 27 March 1999.

He is married to Lyudmila with whom he has two daughters, Katya (1985) and Masha (1986), both of whom were born in Dresden. Lyudmila is also a graduate of Leningrad State University. On leaving university she worked as a stewardess in Kaliningrad and subsequently as a school teacher. In addition to Russian she speaks German, Spanish and French.

The Rt Hon Iain Duncan Smith PC MP
'The Quiet Man"

He was born on 9 April 1954 to Group Captain WGG Duncan Smith and his wife Pamela. His father had had a particularly distinguished career in the RAF and had been awarded the DSO and Bar and the DFC and two Bars.

He was educated at HMS Conway, Cadet School, between 1968 and 1972 before going on to the RMA Sandhurst. In 1975 he was commissioned into the Scots Guards and during his time in the army saw active service in Northern Ireland and Rhodesia as well as spending time in Canada and Germany. Between 1979 and 1981 he was ADC to General Sir John Acland, who was responsible for overseeing Rhodesia's independence.

In 1981, at the age of 27, he left the army and joined GEC-Marconi and in the same year joined the Tory Party becoming a strong supporter of Lady Thatcher. In 1988 he joined Bellwinch plc, a property company based in south-east England, but it was a bad time to be in house building, with the recession biting. He was made redundant and signed on the dole. Luckily, however, in 1989, he secured a position as sales and marketing director for Jane's Information Group, the military publishers, where he remained until 1992.

He cut his political teeth when standing in a by-election in the safe Labour seat of Fulham in 1987. He then contested Bradford West, another safe Labour stronghold, in the 1987 general election before successfully being elected to Parliament to represent Chingford in 1992. In the 1997 general election he was re-elected for the redrawn constituency of Chingford and Wood Green, a seat he continues to hold.

He is a committed Eurosceptic and voted against the Maastricht Treaty in defiance of the then Conservative Prime Minister, John Major. This stand ruled him out of possible promotion from the backbenches whilst John Major remained leader.

In 1997, under William Hague, he joined the Shadow Cabinet and was the Opposition spokesman on Social Security and subsequently on Defence. He also served as a member on Select Committees on Health, on Nolan and on Standards and Privileges.

In September 2001 he was elected Leader of the Conservative Party in the first ever ballot of the Party's membership, previous leaders having been elected by the Party's serving MPs. However, after two years as leader there was a vote of confidence on his leadership called by 25 Conservative MPs, which led to him being forced out of the top job to be replaced by Michael Howard.

Supported by Lord Tebbitt, whose constituency he took over, he was described by him as "a remarkably normal family man with children".

He married his wife, Betsy, the daughter of Lord and Lady Cottesloe, in 1982. They live in a house on her parents' estate at Swanbourne, Buckinghamshire, and have two sons and two daughters.

He is quoted as saying "I do not have all the answers, but I believe that my case for change has something to offer a country sick of government by spin", which is a remarkably honest statement coming from a politician.

The Rt Hon Baroness Betty Boothroyd PC
'Madam Speaker'

Born in Dewsbury, Yorkshire, on 8 October 1929 to Archibald and Mary Boothroyd, both of whom worked in the textile industry. Her education started at local State Schools going on to further study at Dewsbury Technical College of Commerce and Art. In 1946 she worked as a professional dancer and appeared in pantomime in London's West End as a member of the Tiller Girls' chorus line.

As a member of the Labour Party since her teens her continuing interest in politics was soon to take over. She spent time working in the House of Commons as a secretary and political assistant to a number of MPs, including Barbara Castle. She contested parliamentary seats at Leicester South East, in 1957, and Peterborough, in 1959, before travelling to the United States, in 1960, to experience the John Kennedy campaign. She subsequently worked in Washington for two years as a legislative assistant to an American congressman.

Returning to London she continued her work as a secretary and political assistant to various senior Labour politicians and in 1965 succeeded in being elected to Hammersmith Borough Council, where she remained until 1968.

Her aim still being to sit in Parliament, she contested seats in Nelson & Colne, in 1968, and in Rossendale, in 1970, before winning West Bromwich, later named West Bromwich West, as a Labour candidate, in 1973, a position she retained until her retirement in 2000.

She was an active Labour backbencher, very much part of the moderate wing of the party, and in 1974 she was appointed an assistant Government Whip and became an MEP from 1975 to 1977. In 1979 she became a member of the Select Committee on Foreign Affairs, until 1981, and of the Speaker's Panel of Chairmen, until 1987. She was a member of the Labour Party NEC from 1981-1987 and the House of Commons Commission from 1983-1987.

In 1987 she was elected Deputy Speaker of the House of Commons and in 1992 was elected Speaker, the first ever female Speaker. She remained Speaker until her retirement in 2000. Following which she was created a Life Peer, taking on as her title Baroness Boothroyd of Sandwell in the County of West Midlands.

In 1994 she became Chancellor of the Open University, based in Milton Keynes, and has also received a number of honorary degrees from various British Universities. In 2001 her autobiography was published.

She will be remembered best as Madam Speaker where in her final speech to the House she reminded the members of "that famous passage from Ecclesiastes, about there being a time to weep, and a time to laugh; a time to mourn and a time to dance. Well, my dancing days are long past" she said "and I promise the House that I shall not weep, but I shall certainly mourn the fact that an all-important phase in my life has come to a natural end. However, it is time for laughter as well, as we remember all the lighter moments that we have enjoyed together......Therefore I say to you all, in a phrase that you all know too well, but which has never been more true than now: 'Time's up'."

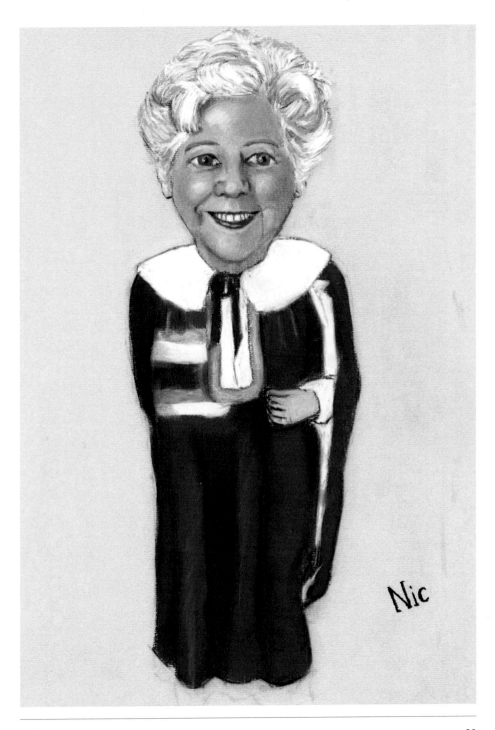

The Rt Hon Michael Howard PC QC MP
'Leader of the Conservative Party'

He was born on 7th July 1941, in South Wales, to Bernard and Hilda Howard. His Father had left Romania between the two World Wars and had established clothes shops in Llanelli and Carmarthen. Michael was educated at Llanelli Grammar School before going on to Peterhouse, Cambridge, where he first read economics before switching to law. At Cambridge he was a contemporary of The Rt. Hon Kenneth Clarke and in 1962 was elected president of the Union.

After graduating he spent a year in the United States where he was introduced to baseball and became a supporter of the Boston Red Socks. He returned to England and in 1964 was called to the Bar.

His first two attempts to enter parliament were in 1966 and 1970 when as a keen football supporter and Liverpool fan he stood as a prospective Conservative candidate for Liverpool Edge Hill. He was chairman of the Bow Group in 1970 and became a QC in 1982.

Whilst he was unsuccessful in his first attempts to be elected to parliament, his fortunes changed on the third try, when he was elected to represent Folkestone and Hythe in Margaret Thatcher's landslide victory in 1983.

He was promoted quickly; in 1984 he became PPS to the Solicitor-General; the following year he became a junior minister in the Department of Trade, responsible for corporate and consumer affairs. In 1987, he moved to the Department of the Environment, first as Minister of State for Local Government and then as Minister of State for Water and Planning. In 1990, he joined the Cabinet as Secretary of State for Employment, abolishing the closed shop and playing a key role in negotiating the UK's opt-out from the Social Chapter at Maastricht.

Following the 1992 election, he was appointed Secretary of State for the Environment and was particularly involved with the Earth Summit in Rio, where he represented the Government.

In May 1993, he became Home Secretary, where he remained for four years, during which time he introduced private prisons and tough mandatory sentences and saw a 15% fall in crime.

After the Tories lost power in 1997, and his unsuccessful bid to become party leader, William Hague appointed him shadow foreign secretary, in which position he is regarded to have performed well up against Robin Cook.

In September 2001 Iain Duncan-Smith was appointed leader of the party and he appointed Michael Howard to the post of Shadow Chancellor of the Exchequer. However, following Mr Duncan-Smith's failure to win enough backing in a confidence vote amongst Tory MPs, Michael Howard was elected, unopposed, in November 2003, to be Leader of the Conservative Party and therefore of Her Majesty's Opposition.

He met his wife, Sandra, a former model, at a Red Cross Ball whom he married in 1975. They have a son, a daughter and a step-son from one of her three previous marriages.

General Colin Powell
'Secretary of State'

He was born on 5 April 1937 in Harlem, New York City, where his father, Luther, was a shipping clerk and his mother, Maud, a seamstress both of whom had emigrated from Jamaica. He was educated in New York, graduating from its City College having obtained a degree in geology. Whilst at college he joined the Army's Reserve Officers' Training Corps where, in 1958, he reached the rank of cadet colonel.

He joined the regular army, was commissioned and sent for duty in West Germany. He was soon sent to Vietnam where he was wounded in action but on his second tour was awarded the 'Soldier's Medal' for pulling several men from a burning helicopter.

In 1971 he received a Master's degree in business administration at the George Washington University. He then worked at the White House, in the Office of Management and Budget before, in 1973, being sent to South Korea to command a battalion beset with racial difficulties. He said "I threw the bums out of the army and put the drug users in jail, the rest, we ran four miles every morning, and by night they were too tired to get into trouble". His regime worked.

After serving in a number of different areas he was appointed, in 1987, National Security Adviser, a post he held for the duration of the Reagan administration. In October 1989 he became the Chairman of the Joint Chiefs of Staff, the highest military position in the Department of Defence. He was the youngest and also the first black person to hold this position. During his tenure he was responsible for the handling of Operation Desert Storm, the operation to remove Saddam Hussein from Kuwait. He retired from this position and the army on 30 September 1993.

Following his retirement from the army, he wrote his memoirs, 'My American Dream', which became a best seller. He also pursued a career addressing audiences both at home and abroad. At the time of the 1996 Presidential elections he was urged to run as a Republican Candidate, but declined. However he did campaign on behalf of the Republican party both at that time and subsequently.

Following the election of George Bush, in 2000, he was made 65th Secretary of State and has taken a leading role in rallying the USA's allies and the United Nations in the war against terrorism. He has come under fire for his role in building the case for the invasion of Iraq and the overthrow of its regime and dictator. Since the removal of Saddam Hussein he has been working to establish an international coalition to assist in the rebuilding of Iraq.

In 1962, while stationed at Fort Devens, Massachusetts, he met and married Alma Johnson with whom he has three children, Michael, Linda and Anne. He is a popular figure throughout the USA and has been honoured with many honorary degrees from universities and colleges. He has also received two Presidential Medals of Freedom, the President's Citizens Medal, the Congressional Gold Medal, the Secretary of State Distinguished Service Medal and the Secretary of Energy Distinguished Service Medal.

Sir Richard Branson
'The Dyslexic Entrepreneur'

Born in the home counties on 18 July 1950 into generations of lawyers, his Father, Ted, was a barrister while his Mother, Eve, focused on ensuring that her three children, Richard, Lindi and Vanessa, were brought up to be very independent.

The one thing about Sir Richard is that he could never be accused of being conventional, save that he spent his early years in the commuter belt at Shamley Green and was sent away to boarding school at Stowe. However, as a dyslexic, a phenomenon hardly acknowledged in the 1960s, he did not excel at the academic side leaving school with one A level in ancient history.

Having started as an entrepreneur selling Christmas trees he moved on whilst still at school, aged 16, to start a national magazine called the Student before setting up a student advisory service. At 20, he founded Virgin, initially as a mail order record retailer but this soon led to him opening his first record shop in Oxford Street, London. At this time he had a slight brush with the law, which taught him early on in his career, that integrity was more important than money or success.

By 1972 he had a recording studio, had signed up his first artist, Mike Oldfield, and the following year Tubular Bells was released. This sold over five million copies and quickly established and underpinned Virgin.

Much to the consternation of his colleagues, who were dead against the idea, in 1984, he started Virgin Atlantic. In spite of British Airways who, under Lord King's stewardship, had pursued a 'dirty tricks' campaign against Virgin, it has become Britain's second largest long-haul international airline. He took on the mantle, which Sir Freddie Laker had started by taking on, fighting and winning against BA.

In 1992 he sold Virgin Music Group to Thorn EMI realising substantial profits, which he was able to plough back into Virgin Atlantic before selling a 49% stake to Singapore Airlines in 1999.

His daring record breaking antics make sure he is kept in the limelight. In 1986 he rekindled the spirit of the Blue Riband, with the fastest recorded crossing of the Atlantic Ocean in his Virgin Atlantic Challenger II. The Blue Riband had gone unchallenged since the SS United States won it in 1952.

A year later, Virgin Atlantic Flyer was the first hot air balloon to cross the Atlantic Ocean, reaching speeds of up to 130mph. In 1991, he crossed the Pacific Ocean, from Japan to Arctic Canada, a distance of 6,700 miles, again breaking all existing records at speeds of up to 245mph. In 1997 his first attempt to circumnavigate the world in a hot air balloon ended shortly after it began but his attempt the following year took him from Morocco to the middle of the Pacific Ocean, travelling 13,700 miles at a maximum height of 37,000 feet.

His tireless energy and entrepreneurship led to him being knighted in 2000, achieved perhaps from his practised belief "that the only way to cope with a cash crisis is not to contract but to expand out of it."

Sir David Lees
'Mr GKN'

Born, in Scotland, on 23 November 1936 to Rear Admiral D M Lees CB DSO. He is the eldest of three sons and unlike his youngest brother, who followed his father into the Royal Navy, also becoming a Rear Admiral, Sir David decided to rebel and qualified as a Chartered Accountant.

He was privately educated at Charterhouse from whence he went on to be an articled clerk with Binder Hamlyn & Co. Hadley Page, an aircraft manufacturer, subsequently offered him a job, where he had been assigned to work by his firm. He was more suited to making and creating, than an audit role of box ticking.

When Hadley Page subsequently went into liquidation he was headhunted, in 1970, by GKN Sankey in Shropshire. GKN is one of Britain's oldest engineering companies whose roots go back to iron works in Wales in the 18th Century.

He worked his way through a number of finance posts within the organisation, before becoming Group Finance Director in 1982; Group Managing Director in 1987; Chairman and Chief Executive in 1988 and then Non-Executive Chairman in 1997 from which post he retired on 20 May 2004.

His 16-year tenure at the top of GKN has been renowned for its steadiness and lack of surprises, always looking to concentrate and build on its core areas. He has steadily built up the car-parts side of the business and has also gradually acquired Westland Helicopters to establish GKN firmly as providers into the aerospace arena.

He is a shy, modest individual but a great team builder; which perhaps is why he has avoided the headlines, as he is surrounded by a strong board, who are not seen as city fat-cats. He has held a number of senior positions, and continues as Non-Executive Chairman of Tate & Lyle, another company with a long history and is Deputy Chairman of Brambles Industries plc. He has been a Director of the Bank of England, Chairman of Courtaulds plc, a member of the Audit Commission and is currently on the Panel on Takeovers and Mergers, to name but a few.

He has strong views on corporate governance, and in particular its demands on senior directors, but he is quite clear, that corporate governance cannot be reduced to mere form filling and box ticking and he feels that the institutional investor has an important part to play in the area of corporate governance generally.

He married Edith Mary Bernard in 1961 and they have two sons and a daughter. His interests include golf, music and the opera. His interest in opera has been rewarded by his appointment as a director of the Royal Opera House, where he is chairman of the Finance and Audit Committee.

Richard Felton
'Generations of Flowers for London'

Born, on 11 August 1950, into a dynasty of florists and horticulturalists, established by his Grandfather, who so impressed the Royal family and their relatives, that the Kaiser, having seen Felton's work, summoned him to 'strike an English note' in the decoration to greet Edward VII, on his visit to Berlin. Felton travelled to Berlin, with 40 staff and 8 tonnes of flowers, for the occasion. Richard was the only grandchild of the grandfather's seven sons. His father died when he was aged 8, having had a distinguished career in the RAF during WWII, including being shot down twice, during Operation Market Garden, an appropriately named operation for a florist!

Finishing his schooling at the Royal Grammar School, Guildford, he decided to follow in the family footsteps. This he did, first by becoming a horticultural and floral apprentice with Thomas Rochford, the largest single house plant nursery in the world, at that time. He worked his way up to the 'Show' Greenhouse tending and preparing the plants for the many shows including the Chelsea and Liverpool shows where the displays gained gold medals.

After 18 months, of gaining a sound knowledge of tropical house plants, he joined Major Eric Roberts, in Cardiff, for two years formal practical and personal training in floristry. This was an excellent grounding on which to return to London in 1972, to join the family business Felton & Sons Ltd, then run by two of his Uncles.

Unfortunately the young Richard did not enjoy working with his Uncles and he was soon persuaded to join a great friend in Paris. There, in a busy flower shop, he quickly became the head decorateur of La Coupole Restaurant, Bvd Montparnasse; the restaurant 'à voir et être vu', the place in which 'to see and be seen'.

Settling into the Parisian life he was able to pursue one of his great hobbies, Napoleonic military history, particularly the 100 days Waterloo campaign. The director general of les Invalides gave Richard personal permission to study from the original manuscripts as long as he did not mention Waterloo! He now has a private collection of thousands of miniature hand painted soldiers and buildings, correctly painted by him as for the Battle of Waterloo.

After three years of running a successful flower shop in the 16th Arrondisement in Paris, his Uncles persuaded him back to London to establish Feltons at Cheapside in the City. This he continued to build up until such time as the Docklands began to take off. He then established Feltons Flowers Ltd, in the heart of Canary Wharf and now has two shops serving the ever increasing masses as they flood into the Docklands. At the same time he still continues to supply many of the City livery companies.

His other great hobbies have been serving with the Territorial Army, the Honourable Artillery Company, based in the City and Cricket; he has been a member of the MCC for over 20 years. Also, with the help of a number of friends, he founded a cricket club, in 1986. It was named the Rhinos, as he claimed 'the members were thick skinned and charged a lot; it was given the motto 'si movet unum ei date' (if it moves, give it one).

He remains a true 'City man', he is a liveryman of the Worshipful Company of Gardeners and in 1997 was President of the Farringdon Ward Club. He married Philippa, in 1990 but the demands of building up Feltons Flowers have sadly led to their recent divorce. Their son, Edward, was born in 1998; perhaps he will keep the family tradition alive.

Sir Ken Morrison CBE
'Mr Supermarkets'

Born on 20 October 1931 he remains at the helm of William Morrison Supermarkets plc, a company established by his father, William, who originally launched the firm as an egg and butter merchant in Bradford. After trading from market stalls for very many years it opened its first shop in Bradford, in 1958.

Having been brought up at the time of rationing, when luxuries were not available and waste was frowned upon, he quickly learnt the value of money and hard work. He thus began working on his father's stall, in Bradford, at the age of seven in order to earn money for those things that he wanted.

He became Chairman and Managing Director of the company in 1956 and whilst he stepped down for a while as Managing Director between 1997 and 2002 he has continued to be Chairman throughout. He has not felt at home in the City and has steadfastly contravened the corporate governance guidelines by refusing to appoint non-executive directors to his board. He only gave way on this at the time of the Safeways takeover at the beginning of 2003. Similarly at that time he took on professional financial PR to help present his bid for Safeways, having never done so before.

In 1961 he opened the company's first supermarket and by 1967 it had become immensely profitable and he floated the company on the London Stock Exchange. At the time the shares were priced at 10 shillings each (50p in today's money) and the issue was 174 times oversubscribed.

The expansion of the company over the years has been almost entirely organic, with the exception of his purchase in 1978 of the Wigan based Whelan's supermarket group from David Whelan, the former Blackburn Rovers footballer. He also, of course, has recently taken over Safeways plc, which has meant an expansion, south, from the company's northern roots. This acquisition resulted in him being voted Sunday Times Business Person of the Year, at the end of 2003.

His hands-on approach, still on occasions to be seen stacking shelves, has meant that he knows the business better than anyone, which has clearly led to its continuing success and expansion. When he has been asked 'what drives him?' his response has been; 'I don't give much regard to personal wealth. I have a nice house and a nice car but I cannot be bothered with silly luxuries. Running the business is what drives me, not the money'. When quizzed about possible retirement he responds 'that he will give up when it stops being fun'.

He was appointed CBE in 1990 and knighted ten years later. His first wife, Edna, sadly died in the early 1990s, with whom he had a son and two daughters. He subsequently married Lynne, and they have a daughter. His eldest daughter, Eleanor, works in the company, but none of his children, as yet, have shown an interest in taking over the helm. His spare time is spent running his sheep farm from his estate in the village of Myton, in North Yorkshire.

Sir John Harvey-Jones MBE
'Troubleshooter'

Born in London on 16 April 1924 to a father who was guardian to a young Maharajah and as a result they lived in tremendous luxury. He attended Tormore School, in Kent before moving on to the Royal Naval College, at Dartmouth, both of which were quite a contrast to his early luxury.

He joined the Royal Navy in 1937 and, having learned German, he went straight into active service at the age of sixteen as a midshipman. It was fortunate that at least he had learned to swim at prep school as, before he was eighteen, he had been torpedoed twice. He then went into submarines, and served in the Mediterranean, Norway, Ceylon and Australia.

In 1945 the Royal Navy sent him to Cambridge, where he learned Russian in six months and became a German and Russian interpreter. In 1952 he was appointed MBE for his work in Naval Intelligence, after a tour of duty commanding an 'E' Boat on what was referred to as 'fishery protection duties in the Baltic'.

He resigned from the Royal Navy in 1956, having reached the rank of Lt. Commander, and joined Imperial Chemical Industries plc (ICI) as a Work Study Officer. Serving in many roles within ICI, he worked his way up the ranks and, in 1973, at the age of 49, he was appointed to the main board before going on, in April 1982, to become Chairman of the company. He held this post until 1987 and changed the fortunes of the company by turning a £200 million loss into a £1000 million profit within three years.

Perhaps one of today's best-known industrialists, he has been on the Boards of many companies including Grand Metropolitan PLC, and was Chairman of the Economist. He has been Chancellor of Bradford University, Vice President of the Royal Society of Arts, a Trustee of the Science Museum, Chairman of the Wild Fowl Trust and a member of The Advisory Council of the Prince's Youth Business Trust, to name but a few.

He has received many awards and was voted Britain's Most Impressive Industrialist. Between 1986 and 1988 he received the title of Industrialist of the Year for three consecutive years and, in 1992, was awarded the title of Motivator of the Year.

I am sure he will be best remembered for his various Troubleshooter television series, in which he managed to give constructive criticism to many companies, including the Morgan Motor Company Limited, who proudly say that 'whilst we definitely took some of his advice we did not take it all by any means'!

When dealing with communication he says: 'Businesses hardly ever communicate enough. Being at the bottom of an organisation is like being at the bottom of a mine – you don't hear anything.' And when talking about dot.coms he says: 'Because I am so bloody old, I've made every mistake in the book. Almost without exception, dot.coms lack a certain maturity in management, mainly because they have not learned from their mistakes.'

In 1947 he married Mary Evelyn Bignall. He is a keen performer in his pony and cart and an enthusiastic cook. He has also found time to write ten books, including two best sellers; 'Making it Happen' and 'Getting it Together'.

The Rt Hon The Lord Mayor Alderman Robert Finch
'676th Lord Mayor of the City of London'

Born in Ootacumund, South India on 20 August 1944 while his father, Brigadier JRG Finch, was on active service in Italy during WWII. He went to Felsted School, in Essex, before going on to study at the College of Law.

He became an articled clerk in his Uncle's firm, Monro Pennefather & Co, qualifying as a Solicitor of the Supreme Court in 1969. At that time he moved to join Linklaters, formerly known as Linklater & Paines, one of the leading firms of solicitors in the City of London, where he has remained ever since.

He was elected a partner of the firm in 1974, specialising in property and real estate and was head of Commercial Real Estate from 1997 to 1999. In that department he worked on many of the major building schemes including the Broadgate development.

He was appointed a director of IFSL, formerly known as British Invisibles, in 2001 and a director of Fleming Family and Partner (Russia) Limited, in 2003. He is also a Church Commissioner, a member of the Council of St Paul's Cathedral, a governor of the College of Law and a trustee of Morden College.

In 1971 he married Patricia Ross and they have two daughters, Alexandra and Isabel. They both have degrees in History of Art; Alexandra works in the National Portrait Gallery and Isabel in the Haywood Gallery. His interest in art will be particularly remembered at Linklaters where he was responsible for starting a modern art collection, which now numbers over 700. His other interests include sailing, which he is able to pursue near to his home in Chichester. He is also a keen skier and hill walker.

He became a Liveryman of the Worshipful Company of Solicitors in 1986 and subsequently Master in 2000. He joined the Worshipful Company of Innholders in 1991 and the Court of that company in 2001. He is also a liveryman of the Worshipful Company of Chartered Surveyors and an Honorary Freeman of the Worshipful Company of Environmental Cleaners. He has an Hon FRICS and a DCL Honoris Causa from City University.

In 1992 he became an Alderman of the City and joined the Court of the Honourable Artillery Company. In 1999 he became Sheriff of the City. The office of Sheriff pre-dates the Norman Conquest and is the oldest in the City.

The role of the Lord Mayor, created in 1192, is the ambassador, both home and abroad for the City of London, and when travelling overseas has the status of a cabinet minister. He is head of the Corporation of London, Chief Magistrate of the City of London and Admiral of the Port of London.

Every year the Lord Mayor raises funds for specific purposes and during this Mayoralty his appeal is to support music, arts education and community programmes under the banner 'Music and the Arts for Everyone'.

He started his mayoralty with a slightly dangerous statement: 'If a Lord Mayor does not make a difference then he's failed.' However, he does not have to eat his words.

Most Rev. and Rt Hon Rowan Williams PC
'First Welsh Archbishop of Canterbury'

Born in Swansea on 14 June 1950, he was Christened, Rowan Douglas. Having been educated at Dynevor Secondary School, he went on to study Theology at Christ's College, Cambridge before moving on to Oxford where he carried out research on Russian Christianity. There he became a Doctor of Philosophy in 1975 and subsequently a Doctor of Divinity in 1989. More recently, in 2003, he received an honorary doctorate of divinity from the University of Wales in recognition of his services to theology.

He went on to spend two years lecturing at Mirfield Theological College, near Leeds. He became a Deacon in 1977 and a Priest the following year before becoming Chaplain, Tutor and Director of Studies at Westcott House, Cambridge. In 1980 he was appointed a lecturer in Divinity at Cambridge prior to becoming Dean and Chaplain at Clare College, Cambridge, in 1984.

In 1986 he moved to Oxford, where he became Canon Residentiary of Christ Church and Professor of Divinity at Lady Margarets. This clearly stood him in good stead for greater things to come as he next moved to be enthroned as the Bishop of Monmouth in 1992, in St Woolos Cathedral, Newport. In 2000 he was enthroned as the Archbishop of Wales and advice he then gave to his bishops was "One of the things you will do as a bishop is to disappoint".

Only two years later he was elected Archbishop of Canterbury on 23 July 2002, and confirmed as 104th Archbishop of Canterbury on 2 December 2002, in St Paul's Cathedral. His enthronement took place on 27 February 2003 in Canterbury Cathedral, his diocesan home. Officially entitled the Most Rev. and Rt Hon. Rowan Williams, with his official residence at Lambeth Palace, opposite the Houses of Parliament.

The Archbishop of Canterbury has many roles, including; Primate of All England, and he is thus responsible for the 13,000 parishes of the Church of England and the Country's senior Christian and spiritual voice. He is also the Diocesan Bishop of Canterbury and leader of the Anglican Communion, the latter includes 38 provinces in communion with the See of Canterbury, a total of some 70 million members throughout the world.

He is a shy, quiet spoken man, with liberal views, who was thrown in at the deep end to address and deal with the issue of homosexual bishops, this he knows "will continue to cause pain and anger and misunderstanding and resentment all round". However, in spite of his quiet manner, he is quite prepared to stand up to anyone for what he believes in, including the Prime Minister, amply demonstrated when he told him "an attack on Iraq would be both immoral and illegal" and subsequently that it was "not a just war", when the UK Government were attempting to justify the steps it had taken.

While Dean of Clare College he was again quite prepared to stand up for what he believed in for, on Ash Wednesday 1985, he was arrested by police armed with sub-machine guns, after clambering over the razor-wire fence at an RAF base, in Cambridgeshire. There, he and his fellow peace protesters, prayed and made a cross of ashes on the runway.

In 1981, he married Jane Paul, a lecturer in theology, whom he met while working in Cambridge. They have a son and a daughter.

Nic

The Dalai Lama XIV
'Spiritual Leader of the Tibetan people'

Named Lhamo Thondup, the Dalai Lama was born on 6 July 1935, to a poor family in Takster in the Tibetan province of Amdo. The Dalai Lama is held to be the reincarnation of each of the previous thirteen Dalai Lamas of Tibet, the first having been born in 1351AD.

When he was barely 3 years old, a search party was sent by the Tibetan government to find the new incarnation of the Dalai Lama. It arrived at Kumbum monastery, led there by a number of signs. One of these concerned the embalmed body of his predecessor, the thirteenth Dalai Lama, who had died aged 57, in 1933. While the body was lying in state, the head was found to have turned from facing south to north-east. Shortly thereafter the Regent, himself a senior lama, had a vision. Looking into the waters of a sacred lake, he saw the letters Ah, Ka and Ma float into view. These were followed by the image of a three storied monastery with a turquoise and gold roof and a path running from it to a hill. Finally he saw a small house with strange shaped guttering. He was convinced that the Ah referred to Amdo, the Ka indicated the monastery at Kumbum, which had three storeys and a turquoise roof.

Searching the neighbouring villages they saw the gnarled branches of juniper in the roof of the Dalai Lama's parents' house and were certain that the new Dalai Lama would be there. Rather than reveal the purpose of their visit, the group asked only to stay the night. The leader of the party, Kewtsong Rinpoche, pretended to be a servant and spent much of the evening observing and playing with the youngest child in the house. The child recognised him and called out Sera lama, which was the leader's monastery.

He was first taken to Kumbum monastery and then in 1939 went on to Lhasa. The following winter he was taken to the Potala Palace and officially installed as the spiritual leader of Tibet. Soon after he went on to Jokhang temple where he was inducted as a novice monk and where he received his education.

In October 1950 news reached Lhasa that an army of 80,000 Chinese soldiers had crossed into Tibet and on 17 November 1950, following strong representations from the Tibetan people, at the age of fifteen, the Dalai Lama was enthroned as the temporal leader of Tibet and its six million people. He appointed two new Prime Ministers, one a monk and the other a lay administrator. They sent delegations to the United States, Great Britain and Nepal to seek assistance but none was forthcoming. They also sent a delegation to China in the hope of negotiating a withdrawal, this too was unsuccessful and he therefore moved to southern Tibet in order to facilitate any flight to exile should the situation deteriorate.

The next nine years saw the Dalai Lama trying to prevent a full-scale takeover of Tibet by China and placating the growing resentment among Tibetan resistance fighters against the Chinese aggressors. However, eventually, in March 1959, the position was such that he had to leave Tibet with about 80 officials. They were given asylum in India and established the Tibetan Government-in-Exile at Dharamsala. They also persuaded the Indian Government to pay for the establishment of Tibetan Education for Tibetan children.

Still remaining in exile, he continues to strive towards the day when he can lead the Tibetan people in exile back to their homeland.

David Beckham OBE
'Creative midfielder'

He was born in Leytonstone, North London, on 2 May 1975, the son of Ted and Sandra Beckham. He was educated in Essex and whilst at school there, aged 11, he won the TSB Bobby Charlton Soccer Skills Award, the start of his award winning career. The prize included a presentation at Old Trafford and a two-week trip to train with Terry Venables' Barcelona side.

After having trials with Leighton Orient and Tottenham Hotspur's school of excellence he signed on as a trainee with Manchester United on 8 July 1991. His team went on to win the FA Youth Cup 1992 and the following season he made his senior team debut in the Coca Cola Cup against Brighton & Hove Albion. On 23 January 1993 he signed on as a Professional for Manchester United.

It was not until September 1994 that he made his next senior appearance, this time against Port Vale in the League Cup; two months later he scored his first goal for United in a match against Galatasary.

In March 1995 Alex Ferguson loaned him to Preston North End, a Third Division club, for a month to gain experience. He played five games and scored twice for them. His first Premiership goal came against Aston Villa in the first game of the 1995/96 season.

The following season, 1996/97, is when he made his name and began to obtain celebrity status. He scored in the Charity Shield match against Newcastle and then went on to score spectacularly, from the half way line, the goal of the season against Wimbledon.

Following these goals he was selected to play in his first match for England against Moldova, and in 2000 he was appointed captain of the England team and, of course, recently led them in Euro 2004, in Portugal, where they were knocked out in the quarter finals. On his own admission his performance at that time had slumped, partly perhaps due to the media speculation over his private life.

He was one of the biggest draws for Manchester United prior to his move to Real Madrid, Spain, in 2003 for a transfer fee of £25 million. Whilst at United, it won the FA Premiership in 1997, 1999, 2000, 2001 and 2003 and, in 1997, it also won the FA Charity Shield and, in 1999, the UEFA Champions League.

He was appointed OBE in 2003 and dedicated it to his team mates and family. He has received numerous awards ranging from Player of the Month in August 1996 to BBC Sports Personality of the Year, in 2001.

He has a number of multi million-pound sponsorship deals recently renewing his contract with Vodafone. He also has deals with Brylcream, Police sunglasses, Pepsi, Marks & Spencer and has entered into a three-year agreement with Gillette, which will see him appearing in advertising throughout the world.

In 1999 he married Victoria Adams, one of the Spice Girls, often referred to as 'Posh Spice'. They were married in Luttrellstown Castle, near Dublin and have two boys, Brooklyn and Romeo.

Muhammad Ali
'Sting like a bee'

Born as Casius Marcellus Clay Jr. on 17 January 1942, in Louisville, Kentucky. Renowned worldwide, not only for his heavy weight boxing, but also for his political activism.

Taking up boxing at the age of 12, he remained an amateur and as such he obtained six Kentucky State Golden Gloves titles, two National Golden Gloves titles, two Amateur Athletic Union titles and ultimately, as an amateur, he won the gold medal in boxing's light heavyweight division of the Rome Olympics in September 1960.

Following this win he turned professional and quickly became famous for his results, self-promotion and unorthodox style; he carried his hands at his sides rather than high to defend his face. Instead, he relied on his very quick reflexes and long reach; he also punched the head much more than most boxers rather than the body.

In 1964, he managed to get an opportunity to fight the heavyweight champion, Sonny Liston. The favourite to win by far was Liston, however, he refused to leave his corner for the eighth round claiming he had an injured shoulder. Casius Clay, as he then was, was duly crowned heavyweight champion of the world. In 1965 he consolidated his position by knocking out Lister in the first round of their rematch.

Between the two matches he became well known for his conversion to Islam and changing his name to Mohammad Ali. In 1966, he refused to serve in the US army in Vietnam, famously saying that he "got nothing against no Viet Cong. No Vietnamese ever called me a nigger". He was stripped of his title and license to box, and sentenced to five years in prison, later over turned on appeal.

In 1970 he was again granted a license to box and started his comeback only to be defeated in 1971 in a long 15 round fight with Joe Frazier, but in 1974 he beat Frazier on points, which entitled him to another shot at the title.

The titleholder at the time was George Foreman, a young undefeated fighter, who had previously demolished Frazier, knocking him out in the second round of their fight. The fight between Ali and Foreman was held in Zaire and promoted as 'The Rumble in the Jungle' and it cemented Ali's reputation as 'The Greatest'. He boxed his best tactical fight, sending Foreman to the floor in the sixth round.

In 1975, he defeated Frazier once more in the 'Thrilla In Manila' and retained the title until he lost to Leon Spinks in 1978, but he soon defeated Spinks in a rematch and became champion for the third time but then vacated the title and retired. The retirement was short lived and in 1980 he challenged Larry Holmes, in what was promoted as 'The Last Hurrah' but lost in the eleventh round. He finally retired in 1981 with a career record of 56 wins, 37 by knockout against only 5 losses.

He was diagnosed with Parkinson's disease in 1982 but has remained a hero to many. He was called upon in 1985 to negotiate the release of kidnapped American citizens in Lebanon and in 1996 he lit the Olympic flame in Atlanta, Georgia. During those Olympics he was also presented with a replacement gold medal having thrown the previous one in the Ohio River after being refused service in a restaurant because of his race.

Paula Radcliffe MBE
'Marathon Woman'

Britain's top long distance runner of her time. Born on 17 December 1973 in Cheshire, the elder of two children born to Peter and Patricia, a brewery executive and headmistress respectively, both keen runners. As a child she would watch her father train for marathons and sometimes accompany him for short distances. Competing was in her blood as her great aunt, Charlotte Radcliffe, won an Olympic swimming silver medal at 4x100m relay in 1920.

At the age of nine she joined the Frodsham Harriers where she did well both at track and field events. However, at the age of eleven, the family moved to live in Bedford where she joined the Bedford County Athletics' Club. She left school with four grade A, A levels and went on to Loughborough University where, in 1996, she obtained a first class honours degree in European Studies majoring in business and languages, she is fluent in French and German.

She won her first major championship in 1992, the World Junior Cross Country Championship, in Boston. The previous year she had come in 15th in the same category when the championship was held in Antwerp. In 1995 she finished fifth in the Gothenburg World Championships over 5,000 metres.

In the 1996 Olympics, in Atlanta, she again came 5th but improved to 4th in the 1997 World Championships. A year later she won the 10,000 metres at the 1998 World Championships. Her first major track medal came with a silver in the 10,000 metres at the 1999 World Championships, in Seville.

She finished in fourth place in the 10,000 metres at the 2000 Olympic Games in Sydney but after winning the World Half-Marathon Champion-

ships in 2000 and 2001 and the 2001 World Cross Country Championship she realised her real strength came in long distance running.

In 2002 she came first in eight races including the London and Chicago Marathons. In 2003 she successfully defended her title to the London Marathon, improving on her previous world-record time by nearly two minutes.

Her extremely positive attitude, her absolute determination and her disciplined perseverance have meant that not only has she achieved success on the track but at the same time has achieved academic success. Her attitude is that by putting in the work one will achieve results, all this in spite of the fact that she suffers from exercise-induced asthma.

Whilst she is sometimes accused of being one of the nicest people in athletics, she is not afraid of standing up for her beliefs and being outspoken on the question of sporting cheats.

She was elected as British Female Athlete of the year in 1999, 2001 and 2002 and was appointed MBE in June 2002. She was the IAAF World Female Athlete of 2002. On 15 April 2000 she married Gary Lough, also a distance runner.

Finally, during 2004 she has spent her time preparing for the Olympics in Athens and there we have recently seen her sadly pull out shortly before the end of the hugely challenging marathon.

Sir Clive Woodward OBE
'English Rugby'

He was born on 6 January 1956 in Ely, Cambridgeshire, and educated at HMS Conway, the naval boarding school, in Anglesey. He went to Loughborough University where he graduated with a degree in Sports Science, before going on to obtain a Post-Graduate Certificate of Education.

In 1979, following university, he joined Rank Xerox on a graduate trainee scheme whilst at the same time playing rugby for the Leicester Tigers. In 1980 he won the first of his 21 England caps and toured with the Lions in both 1980 and 1993.

In 1984 he became the Midlands regional manager for Xerox but left in 1985 to emigrate to Australia to take up a post as National Sales Director for Portfolio Leasing, a wholly owned subsidiary of the Ford Motor Company. He continued his love of rugby while in Australia and captained the Sydney Premier Grade side, Manly.

He returned to England in 1990 and established, with a partner, their own leasing company, Sales, Finance and Leasing Limited. He sold out this successful business to his partner, which enabled him to focus exclusively on English Rugby.

On his return to England, rather than playing, he turned his attention to coaching and presided over Henley RFC's success in the early 90s where they gained three promotions in as many years. He followed this by coaching first the London Irish in 1995, steering them to promotion to the Premiership and secondly Bath. He also spent time coaching the England Under 21s for three seasons, from 1994 to 1997.

In September 1997, whilst at Bath, he was offered the opportunity of becoming the first professional, full-time coach of the England Rugby Union Team. Naturally, he accepted. His attention to detail and his absolute determination, desire and focus to establish England as the best, most successful rugby playing nation in the world has paid off.

He led England to victory, winning the Grand Slam in the Six Nations Championship in 2003 and later that year led the team into the nail-biting final of the World Cup, which was eventually won in extra time by the drop goal from the boot of Jonny Wilkinson.

He is a strong believer in the similarities between running a business and a sports team and is quoted as saying "There's a complete parallel. Running a successful company you need the same skills as you do to run a successful sports team. I make no apology that I've brought my business background into play".

His recent decision to leave rugby and turn his attention to a new career has surprised many.

He was appointed OBE in 2002 for his services to Rugby Union and Knighted following his team's successful win of the 2003 World Cup.

Nic

Jonny Wilkinson OBE
'The Boot'

Currently one of the most highly rated English rugby players, dedicated, focused modest and complimentary of his fellow team members. He was born in Frimley, Surrey, on 25 May 1979 to a rugby-playing father, Phil, and his wife, Philippa.

He was educated at Pierrepont, Frensham, before going on to Lord Wandsworth College, in Hampshire, and as a schoolboy, in addition to rugby, he played cricket and tennis to a very high standard. The England rugby selectors noticed him when he was part of the English 18s Schools tour of Australia in 1997 where he scored 94 points in only 5 games. He joined Newcastle Falcons and signed a two-year contract with them, having turned down a place at Durham University. His elder brother, Mark, also has a contract with Newcastle Falcons, as a fitness trainer.

In 1998, at the age of 18, he played his debut for England, as a replacement for Mike Catt, in England's win over Ireland, at Twickenham, which sealed England's win of the Triple Crown. He was then chosen for the 1998 summer tour of Australia, known as the 'Tour of Hell', in which, on his first occasion as fly-half, England was defeated by 76 points.

In February 1999 he was again called up for the England team for the Five Nations match against Scotland. He was given the opportunity to play at centre and to kick at goal, owing to the fact that Will Greenwood had been injured. In the first three matches he kicked 16 out of 17 attempts and scored all of England's points in the match against Ireland, with seven penalties.

By the final match of that Five Nations series further injuries to others resulted in him taking the place of Paul Grayson, as fly-half against Wales. Later that year in the 1999 Rugby World Cup he

scored 32 points in England's 67-8 massacre of Italy, but was not chosen when South Africa beat England in the quarter-final.

His next couple of years saw him consolidate his strengthening position in the England team, surpassing Rob Andrew's points record and ensuring his position for the all-important 2003 Rugby World Cup. 2003 started well for England in the RBS Six Nations Championship with England winning the Grand Slam in which, in their final match, they beat Ireland, in Dublin, 42-6.

The highlight of the year, however, came at the time England reached the final of the 2003 Rugby World Cup when, in extra time, with the score 17-17, he kicked a spectacular drop-goal to win the cup for England, 20-17.

Appointed MBE in the New Years Honours of January 2003 for his services to Rugby, a year later he was appointed OBE in recognition of his part in England's dramatic World Cup victory in Australia. He was also awarded the 2003 BBC Sports Personality of the Year, the International Rugby Board Player of the Year and the International Players' Player of the year, having also received that award the previous year, in 2002. Following his return to Newcastle, in December 2003, he sustained a shoulder injury, which kept him away from rugby until his return to action, to play for the Newcastle Falcons, in August 2004.

Tim Henman OBE
'English Tennis'

He was born on 6 September 1974, in Oxford, to parents Tony and Jane. It is not surprising that he has become a tennis player as his father played tennis to county standard and both his grandfather and great grandmother had played at Wimbledon. His grandfather was Henry Billington, who reached the third round in 1948, 1950 and 1951.

Tim first played tennis at the age of three and by five was already focused on making tennis his career. He started his schooling at the local primary at Weston on the Green before going on to the Dragon School, Oxford. At 11 he received a Slater Scholarship and went on to Reeds School at Cobham.

Jim Slater, the financier, had established the scholarship scheme together with David Lloyd, the former British Davis Cup player. This scholarship initiative was aimed to improve the coaching of young British tennis players. After a full day of schooling they would go to one of the David Lloyd indoor tennis centres to be coached for three hours.

He left school at 16, following his GCSEs, in order to concentrate on his tennis career. In 1992, he won the under 18 British National Junior Singles title before joining 'the Tour' in 1993. Over the ensuing years he rose steadily through the rankings, breaking into the Top 200 in 1994, the Top 100 in 1995 and the Top 30 in 1996.

This was the time of his real breakthrough, becoming Britain's No 1, reaching the quarterfinals at Wimbledon and the semi-finals of six ATP tournaments. At the end of that year he was rewarded for his efforts by winning the 'Most Improved Player' at the ATP Tour Awards.

In January 1997, in Sydney, he won his first ATP tournament but he was then put out of action for 7 weeks by surgery to his elbow. However, this did not prevent him from reaching the quarterfinals of Wimbledon. Also that year he received the runner-up prize in the BBC Sports Personality of the Year awards.

In 1998, he reached the semi-finals at Wimbledon and won ATP titles in Tashkent and Basel. As a result of his improved performance and consistency he reached No7 in the world. In 2000 he reached the 4th round at Wimbledon and won ATP titles in Brighton and Vienna.

2001 saw him back in the semi-finals at Wimbledon and winning ATP titles in Copenhagen, Basel and Adelaide. In 2002, he again reaches the Wimbledon semi-finals, but in both 2003 and 2004 he was knocked out in the quarter-finals. He did, however, in 2003, win the ATP titles in Paris and Washington DC, but his time at the Olympics, in Athens 2004 were short-lived, being knocked out in the first round. He was appointed OBE in the New Years Honours list in 2004.

He married Lucy on 11 December 1999 and they have a daughter Rosie who was born on 19 October 2002. His interests include all sports but in particular golf in which he plays off a handicap of four and football where he supports Oxford United.

Nasser Hussain OBE
'Reviver of English Cricket'

He was born on 28 March 1968 in Madras, India to an Indian father, Jawad (anglicised to Joe) and an English mother, Shireen. They had met when Joe, who had an electronics business in India, was visiting the UK. His early years were spent on the boundary at the Chepauk stadium in Madras, where he watched his father play. The family moved to Ilford when he was six and at that time he became an excellent leg-spin bowler.

He attended the Forest School, in Snaresbrook and managed to obtain ten O levels and three A levels, in addition to being the youngest ever player to represent Essex Under-11 Schools, when he was eight and Under-15 Schools, when he was twelve. Already with his prowess in cricket he could have gone straight onto the staff at Essex but his father insisted he went to University and only play for the county during the vacation. He went to Durham to study geo-chemistry for his Natural Sciences BSc.

In 1987 he made his debut for Essex. In 1993 he won Essex player-of-the-year award and in 1996 was appointed their vice-captain. In April 1999 he was appointed the Essex captain but hands over to Ronnie Irani a year later so that he could concentrate on his duties to the England team.

In 1990 he was chosen for the England tour of the West Indies and will be remembered for playing both the innings of the fifth test in Antigua with a broken wrist, which put him out of action for much of the following season. He was recalled again to play for England for the last four Tests of the Ashes Series in 1993.

In 1996 he was recalled again and scored his maiden Test century playing against India as No 3. Another century followed at Trent Bridge and he was named vice-captain of the England tour-

ing team for that winter. The following year he recorded his highest Test score, 207 against the Australians, including three successive fours off the bowling of Shane Warne.

He took over from Alec Stewart as captain of the England team in July 1999 after a disappointing performance in the 1999 World Cup. Under his captaincy England won four Test series in a row for the first time since Mike Brearly, rose to third place in the ICC Test Championship table and was rewarded by being appointed OBE in January 2002 for his successful captaincy of the England team and the revival of English cricket.

After a disappointing 2003 World Cup performance he stepped down, in March 2003, as one-day captain and in July stepped down as Test captain, handing over to Michael Vaughan. He retired from all cricket in May 2004 and signed a four-year contract with Sky Sports, joining their commentary team for the NatWest Series against New Zealand and the West Indies.

Whilst at Durham he met his wife, Karen. They were married in 1993 and have two children. She became a teacher but gave that up in 1999 to be able to spend time on tour with her husband.

Joanne K Rowling OBE
'Harry Potter Creator'

She was born on 31 July 1965, in the Chipping Sodbury General Hospital. Her father, was a Rolls-Royce engineer and her mother, Anne, a school laboratory technician. She had a sister, Di, two years her junior who from an early age listened for hours to her elder sister's story telling.

She was brought up at Tutshill, near Chepstow, in the Forest of Dean where she attended Tutshill Primary School, which she hated. She was scared of her teacher and everything about the school was old fashioned, including the inkwells. She went on to Wyedean Comprehensive and kept her story telling going, with serials at lunchtime. In her final year she was made head girl. After this she went straight to Exeter University graduating, in 1986, with a degree in French and Classics.

On leaving University she became a secretary, but on her own admission, accepts that she was not a particularly good one as she is a very disorganised person and was more interested in writing stories and notes and ideas for her stories than her job as a secretary.

Following the death of her mother, who sadly died in 1990, at the age of 45, she went to Portugal to teach English as a foreign language and it was whilst she was there, in about 1995, that she started planning the Harry Potter series. From the outset she planned seven books and very early on had already written the final chapter of the seventh book.

She returned to the UK with a suitcase of notes for her Harry Potter series and went to live near her newly married sister, in Edinburgh. There she survived on welfare benefit while training for a full teaching certificate. However she did not take up teaching until she had finished her first book and had started the long task of trying to find a publisher. When the first book was published it enabled her to give up teaching and to concentrate on her writing.

Five of the seven books have now been published and naturally the sixth is eagerly awaited. The first, Harry Potter and the Philosopher's Stone, was published in 1997 and very quickly became a best seller. A year later came Harry Potter and the Chamber of Secrets followed the next year by Harry Potter and the Prisoner of Azkaban.

In 2000, book four of the series was published, Harry Potter and the Goblet of Fire, but then there was a long wait until book five was eventually published in 2003, Harry Potter and the Order of the Phoenix. The books have all been best sellers and are gradually being turned into films, which see record attendances.

In 1992, she married Jorge Arantes, a Portuguese journalist, whom she met while working in Portugal but they divorced on her return to the UK. They had a daughter Jessica. She subsequently married, her second husband, a GP, Dr Neil Murray, on 26 December 2001. They have a son, David, born in March 2003 and they are expecting another child due in 2005. We are assured that this addition will not delay the publication of book No 6.

She was appointed OBE in 2000 and became a Fellow of the Royal Society of Literature in 2002. She has won many awards for her writing including Author of the Year, British Book Awards, 2000.

Dick Francis CBE
'Jockey, Journalist, Author'

Born on 31 October 1920 in Lawrenny, Pembrokeshire, South Wales, but then moved to Maidenhead where he attended the Maidenhead County Boys School. The son of George, a jockey, and Catherine, he was a keen horseman while still at school and won many awards.

In 1940 he joined the Royal Air Force for the remainder of World War II finishing his time as a Lancaster bomber pilot having initially trained on Spitfires. Following the war he became an Amateur National Hunt Jockey before turning professional in 1948 and very soon became well known in the world of British National Hunt racing.

He won more than 350 races, was Champion Jockey in the 1953/54 race season, and was retained as jockey to Her Majesty Queen Elizabeth the Queen Mother for four seasons from 1953 to 1957. Every year he would sign a copy of his new novel and have it delivered, hot off the press, to Clarence House.

He was a jockey on eight occasions in the Grand National Steeplechase and very nearly won in 1956, when his horse, the Queen Mother's 'Devon Loch' collapsed 40 yards from the winning post.

In 1957 he gave up racing professionally after another serious fall and completed his autobiography, 'The Sport of Queens', which was published later that year. He also joined the Sunday Express where he worked as the racing correspondent for sixteen years.

Whilst at the Sunday Express he started his fiction writing, publishing his first novel, Dead Cert, in 1962. He produced a best selling novel every year since until he gave up writing in 2001, following the death of his wife. 'Forfeit', in 1968,

'Whip Hand', in 1979 and 'Come to Grief, in 1995 each won an Edgar Allen Poe Award for best novel from the Mystery Writers of America, the only author to win more than one of this prestigious award.

In addition to his novels and autobiography he has written the biography of Lester Piggott, 'A Jockey's Life', and eight short stories. He was appointed OBE, in 1984 and subsequently CBE, in 2000. He has received many awards including Silver, Gold and Diamond Dagger awards from the Crime Writers Association. In 1991 he was awarded an Honorary Doctorate of Humane Letters by Tufts University, Massachusetts and in 1996 was created Grand Master by the Mystery Writers of America, for his life's work.

In 1947 he married Mary Benchley with whom he had two sons and over fifty years of happy married life. She had helped him with his writings, particularly on the research side. She sadly died in 2000 and following her death he published his 39th, and final novel, Shattered, in 2001.

Nic

Halle Berry
'Hollywood Star'

Named after the Halle Brothers department store, she was born on 14 August 1968 in Cleveland Ohio to an African American Father and a white mother, a psychiatric nurse, by whom she was raised following her parents' divorce when she was aged four.

She first appeared in the spotlight at the age of 17 as the winner of the Miss Teen All-American Pageant. It was after this that she became a model and then achieved her first professional acting role in the television series Living Dolls. She next appeared in Knots Landing prior to winning her first big-screen role in Jungle Fever in 1991. In the same year she appeared with Bruce Willis and Damon Wayne in The Last Boy Scout.

In Boomerang in 1992 she played as Eddie Murphy's "love interest" and also received rave reviews for her performances in the title role of Alex Haley's television mini-series, Queen, as a young woman struggling against the brutal conditions of slavery. 1992 also saw her marry the baseball player, David Justice, but this tumultuous marriage ended in an acrimonious divorce in 1996.

Perhaps her first world-renowned debut occurred in 1994 in her comic performance as Sharon Stone, the sexy, scheming secretary in the live version of The Flintstones. The following year she was back, in a more serious role, in the adoption drama Losing Isaiah, for which the critics gave a mixed reception. In this she starred opposite Jessica Lange as a former crack addict battling to win custody of her child, who had been adopted as a baby by an affluent white couple.

Following this she played in a number of mediocre films including Executive Decision, Rich Man's Wife and B*A*P*S*, until in 1998 she received rave reviews when she starred in Warren Beatty's Bullworth, as a street wise young woman coming to the aid of a bumbling politician.

In 1999 she won an Emmy and Golden Globe for her role in the cable movie, Introducing Dorothy Dandridge, which she co-produced and the following year starred as Storm in Bryan Singer's very successful adaptation of The X-Men. Dominic Sena's Swordfish with John Travolta, which was touted as the first film to feature Berry baring her breasts was not such a success. The following time she pursued this course however was in Monster's Ball in 2001, a romantic drama directed by Marc Forster in which she starred as a woman who becomes involved with a racist ex-cop, Billy Bob Thornton, who oversaw the prison execution of her husband, Sean Combs. Berry earned wide praise and was nominated for a Golden Globe and won the Oscar for Best Actress.

January 2001 saw Berry marry again this time to Eric Benet but unfortunately this marriage too has proved difficult, leading to a further divorce.

With another brilliant performance this time, as Jinx, in Die another Day in 2002 she firmly established herself amongst the Bond stars. X2, Gothika and Catwoman all go to establish Berry as an icon of her era, perhaps best summed up by her speech at the Oscars with her words "this moment is for Dorothy Dandridge, Lena Horne......and its for every nameless, faceless woman of colour that now has a chance because the door tonight has been opened".

Sir Peter Ustinov CBE
'The Prolific Raconteur'

Born on 16 April 1921 to Jona (known as Klop) and Nadia. Principally of wealthy Russian blood but with a smattering of German, Spanish, French, Italian and Ethiopian mixed in. His grandfather was exiled from Russia for refusing to take an oath to the Eastern Orthodox Church, as he was a Protestant. Klop, his father, served in the German army in the First World War starting as a private soldier but he soon was commissioned into the Air Force.

Sir Peter died on 28 March 2004, at the age of 82, having, in the words of his biographer, John Miller, ".. had enough careers for about six other men. He was phenomenally busy". When he was asked what would be his ideal epitaph, he responded, with his usual quick wit and good humour, 'Keep off the grass'.

He was always a man of laughter, quotes, anecdotes and stories such as, 'Her virtue was that she said what she thought, her vice, that what she thought didn't amount to much' or perhaps the one most applicable to him 'The point of living, and being an optimist, is being foolish enough to believe that the best is yet to come'.

By the age of 19 he was already an actor and playwright and at 25 he directed his first film, 'School for Secrets', which he had also written. He wrote his first play, 'House of Regrets' in 1940, which was performed in 1942 and went on to write a further 22 plays, 13 books, nine films and very many memoirs.

His first major success as a playwright was with his 'The Love of Four Colonels', in 1951 and perhaps his next most successful was 'Romanoff and Juliet', in 1956, which he subsequently acted and directed. Whilst he was writing plays he also managed to find the time to act, both on the stage and for the cinema. He had his first Oscar nomination in 1951 when acting Nero, in 'Quo Vadis', and later won two Oscars for best supporting actor first as a slave-trader in 'Spartacus', in 1960 and secondly as a tourist guide, who becomes mixed up with gangsters, in 'Topkapi', in 1964.

In January 1942 he was called up and posted to the Royal Sussex Regiment, before becoming a runner in South-Eastern Command. Later he appeared before the War Office Selection Board where it was stated 'on no account is this man to be put in charge of others'. He remained a private but to compensate for this he was made batman to Lt Col David Niven, who arranged for him to be issued with a pass stating "this man may go anywhere, and do anything at his discretion in the course of duty".

In 1971 he became a Goodwill Ambassador for UNICEF, and in 1978 was given its award for Distinguished Service and in 1995, its International Child Survival Award. In 1975 he was appointed CBE and in 1990, knighted in the Birthday Honours. In 1992 he became Chancellor of the University of Durham.

In 1940 he married Isolde Denham with whom he had a daughter, Tamara, in 1945. They had been apart from one another for most of the war and their marriage came to an end when Isolde announced that she wished to marry a journalist, Derek Dempster. They therefore divorced in 1950. He subsequently married, in 1954, Suzanne Cloutier, a French Canadian actress who had played Desdomona in Orson Welles's film, Othello. Together they had a son, Igor and two daughters, Pavla and Andrea. They were divorced in 1971 and the following year he married Hélène du Lau D'Allemans, at a secret ceremony in Corsica.

Nic

Rowan Atkinson
'Black Adder'

Actor and writer, who started his acting career in the Oxford Revue's show at the Edinburgh Fringe Festival in 1977. He was born on 6 January 1955 in Newcastle-upon-Tyne, to Eric and Ella, owners of a farm where he grew up together with his two elder brothers, Rupert and Rodney. He attended the Cathedral Chorister School in Durham then St Bees School before going on to Newcastle and Oxford Universities where he obtained a degree in Electrical Engineering.

During his time at Oxford he met the screen-writer, Richard Curtis, with whom he wrote and performed comedy revues, which led to him co-writing and performing in "Not the Nine O'clock News" in 1979. This won an International Emmy Award and Rowan Atkinson won the 'British Academy Award': 'Best Light Entertainment Program of 1981'. He was also named as 'BBC Personality of the Year' for these perform-ances. However even before that, in 1978, he was already on stage in London, in 'Beyond a Joke' at Hampstead.

By 1983 he had established himself as Black Adder in which he played Edmund, the younger son of Richard IV, set in 1485-95. Black Adder II saw him as a Lord in Queen Elizabeth's court, while Black Adder III had him as a butler to the Prince Regent, Hugh Laurie, set in 1760 to 1815. Black Adder IV or Black Adder Goes Forth was set in the World War 1 trenches where he played a Cap-tain on the Western Front in 1917. In each series, his role was consistently hampered by his inept servant Baldrick, Tony Robinson. For his appear-ances in Black Adder Goes Forth he received the award of the Best Light Entertainment Perform-ance at the British Academy Award 1990.

In the 1990's his success really came from his crea-tion of the Mr Bean character, the clumsy, gorm-less walking disaster. Between 1990 and 1995 he produced 13 special 25 minute programmes which were released by the BBC from time to time starting with 'Mr Bean' and the 'Return of Mr Bean' and ending with 'Tee Off, Mr Bean' and 'Goodnight Mr Bean'. For his performances as Mr Bean he has received many awards, includ-ing, a BAFTA for Best Light and Entertainment Performer and the Golden Rose at Montreux.

In addition to Black Adder and Mr Bean he has been prolific in his performances which include parts in; Peter Cook & Co (1980); Dead On Time (1982); the unofficial James Bond film, Never Say Never Again (1983); The Tall Guy (1989); Four Weddings and a Funeral (1994); The Thin Blue Line (1995); Scooby-Doo (2002); Johnny English (2003) and Love Actually (2003) to mention but a few.

He made many contributions to Comic Relief and appeared as the 9th Doctor; in the 1999 Doctor Who spoof 'The Curse Of Fatal Death', but his performances as an inept British secret service official, Latham, in the Barclaycard commercials, with his more efficient colleague Bough, will live on.

Marrying Sunetra Sastry, a make-up artist, in 1990, where Stephen Fry was his best man. They have two children, a girl, Lily and a boy, Ben-jamin. His HGV licence is not required for his hobby of driving round the tennis court in his go-karts, but his interest in fast cars takes him racing his Aston Martins in the Aston Martins Owners Club, where he has been known to crash!

Nic

Sir Michael Caine CBE
'You were only supposed to blow the bloody door off!'

Born Maurice Joseph Micklewhite on 14 March 1933 in Bermondsey, London. His father was a fish-porter at Billingsgate and his mother a charwoman. He went to school at Wilson's Grammar following his return to London after WWII. At 14, he was introduced, for the first time, to amateur dramatics, by a Methodist minister.

At 16, he left school and after struggling in several low paid jobs, he eventually joined the army as a private soldier to do his National Service. He was posted to Korea with the Royal Fusiliers. Following his discharge, in 1953, he began acting in regional and repertory theatre taking the stage name Michael Scott but later changed this to Michael Caine, after the film 'The Caine Mutiny' starring Humphrey Bogart.

In 1964 he had his big break. After ten years of bit parts and small roles he was cast as Lt Bromhead in the film 'Zulu'. He had actually applied for the role of Private Hook but that had already gone to James Booth. Shortly after the release of Zulu Harry Saltzman approached him, to star in 'The Ipcress File' which was released in 1965. This was the first of the espionage trilogy, followed by 'Funeral in Berlin', in 1966 and 'The Billion Dollar Brain', in 1967.

He has now appeared in over 100 films, his first being in 1956, 'A Hill in Korea', which was not a resounding success. His ability to be serious or humorous has meant that he has never been idle and has appeared continuously in films since then including 'Alfie', in 1966, 'The Italian Job' in 1969, where the Mini was put through it's paces. In 1975 he gave one of his best performances in a partnership with Sean Connery, in John Huston's, 'The Man Who Would Be King' in which Shakira also had a role.

Still as active as ever, if not even more so, in 2000, he was in four films, 'Shiner', 'Quills', 'Get Carter' and 'Miss Congeniality'. Next, in 2001, he was in two films, 'Last Orders' and 'Quicksand'. The following year he was in 'The Quiet American' and 'Austin Powers in Goldmember' and in 2003, 'The Actors', 'Secondhand Lions' and 'The Statement'. In 2004 he was in 'Around the Bend' and 'The Weatherman' and so it goes on and on.

He has also written his autobiography, 'What's It All About', in 1992, and a number of other books including 'Not Many People Know That', in 1985, 'Not Many People Know This Either', in 1986, 'Moving Picture Show', in 1988 and 'Acting in Film', in 1990.

In addition he has also appeared in a number of mini series for television including 'Jack The Ripper', in 1988, 'Jekyll and Hyde', in 1990, 'World War II - When Lions Roared', in 1994 and '20,000 Leagues under the Sea', in 1997.

He met his first wife, Patricia Haines, when they were both acting in repertory, they were married in 1955 but subsequently divorced. They had a daughter Nikki. He later married, in 1973, Shakira Baksh, a former Miss Guyana, and they have a daughter Natasha. He was appointed CBE in 1992 and knighted in 2000. He has also been awarded two Oscars, two BAFTAs and three Golden Globes. His interests naturally include the cinema, theatre and travel but also gardening.

Pierce Brosnan
'Agent 007'

Born on 16 May 1953 in Navan, Ireland, his father, Thomas, was a carpenter who left his mother, May, when he was just a year old. His mother then travelled to London to train as a nurse, leaving him to be brought up by her parents. Unfortunately, when he was six, both his grandparents died and he then stayed with other relatives and in lodgings.

At 11 he came to join his mother in England going to school at Elliott Comprehensive, here he suffered bullying for being Irish. He soon learnt to change his accent so as to blend in more with his peers.

In spite of his success at both art and English he left school at 16 and began training to be a commercial artist in a photographic studio. Encouraged by a work mate he joined the Kennington Oval House Theatre Club which led him towards the acting world. He left his work to pursue this career. To do this he worked at various jobs from cab driver to fire-eater in a circus.

In 1973 he enrolled at the Drama Centre of London graduating in 1976 at which time he became acting assistant stage manager at the Theatre Royal, in York. He made his professional stage debut in 'Wait until Dark' and was spotted by the playwright, Tennessee Williams, and cast as McCabe in 'Red Devil Battery Sign' at the Roundhouse. In 1977 he moved on to Noel Coward's Semi-Monde. His performances of 'Red Devil Battery Sign' had been seen by the director, Franco Zeffirelli, who cast him opposite Joan Plowright in his production of 'Filumena'.

In 1980 he made his cinema debut with a small part in 'The Long Good Friday', starring Bob Hoskins. He has also had a number of television appearances including 'The Manions of America'

series, in 1981; the title role in the 'Remington Steele' series, between 1982 and 1987; 'Nancy Astor', in 1984; 'Noble House', in 1988; 'Around the World in 80 Days', in 1989 and 'Robinson Crusoe', in 1996.

He married Cassandra Harris, an actress, who was a Bond Girl, in 'For Your Eyes Only'. It was while she was filming on Corfu, in 1980, that the Bond producer, Cubby Broccoli, noticed Pierce as a potential Bond. It took until 1995 before he appeared as James Bond in Goldeneye. Two years later 'Tomorrow Never Dies' was released and he continued as Bond in 1999 in 'The World is Not Enough' and in 2002 'Die Another Day'.

In addition to his stardom in Bond he has appeared in a number of other films, including; 'Nomads', in 1986; 'The Forth Protocol', in 1987; 'The Deceivers', in 1988; 'Mr Johnson', in 1991; 'Lawnmower Man', in 1992; 'Mrs Doubtfire', in 1993; 'Love Affair', in 1994; 'The Mirror has Two Faces', in 1996; 'The Nephew', in 1998, where he was also the producer as he was in 'The Thomas Crown Affair', in 1999. He was also in 'Grey Owl', in 2000 and 'The Taylor of Panama', in 2001.

Sadly his wife, Cassandra, died of cancer, in 1991, they had a son, a stepson and a stepdaughter. Subsequently, in 2001, he married Keely Shaye Smith, whom he had met when she intervened him in 1994 for 'Entertainment Tonight'. They have two sons. He is a man who is particularly interested in the welfare of children and as such is an Ambassador for the Prince's Trust and a Patron of Irish UNICEF.

Jennifer Aniston
'Rachel Green'

She was born on 11 February 1969 at Sherman Oaks, in California of Greek ancestry, and spent part of her early life in Greece. Her family name was Anastassakis but her parents on the advice of her godfather, Telly Savalas, changed that to Aniston. When her father, John, landed a role in the daytime soap, 'Love of Life' she moved across to New York. Shortly after their arrival in New York, when she was nine, her parents separated and her mother, Nancy, a model and occasional actress, then brought her up.

Her first taste of acting occurred when, at 11, she joined the Rudolph Steiner School's Drama Club. She later went on to study at the New York High School for Performing Arts, from which she graduated in 1987, with the aim of going into showbiz.

Her attempts to 'make it in showbiz' took some time. At first all she was offered were a few roles in off-Broadway productions, including 'For Dear Life' and 'Dancing on Checker's Grave'. During this period, like many budding stars, in order to make ends meet she spent time waitressing. However in 1989, she landed her first television role as a regular on the series 'Molly'. She also appeared in regular roles in 'The Edge' and 'Ferris Bueller', she had a recurring part on 'Herman's Head' and guest roles on series such as 'The Larry Sanders Show', 'Partners', 'Burke's Law' and 'Quantum Leap'. She credits her first steps into television to following her agent's advice, namely to lose thirty pounds.

Her real break came when she was asked to audition for the role of Monica in the new TV series 'Friends Like These' subsequently shortened to 'Friends'. She declined but asked in stead to play the part of Rachel Green, which part she was given. From 1994, the first appearance of Friends, until 2004, the showing of the final series, her face became one of the best-known faces on television as she portrayed Rachel Green.

In addition to the long running series of Friends, she has also found time to appear in a number of films including: 'She's the One', in 1996, where she was Renee Fitzpatrick; 'Picture Perfect', in 1997, as Kate Mosley; 'Til There Was You, also in 1997, as Debbie; 'The Object of My Affection', in 1998, as Nina Borowski; 'The Good Girl', in 2002; 'Bruce Almighty', a year later, as Grace, and 'Along Came Polly' in 2004, where she played Polly Prince.

She has received and been nominated for a great number of awards, principally, but by no means exclusively, for her role in Friends, including winning a Golden Globe in 2003 and an Emmy in 2002.

In July 2000, she married her long-term boy friend, and similar megastar, Brad Pitt; they currently live in Los Angeles. In her spare time she enjoys hiking and camping and things that take her closer to nature, she also enjoys painting and at the age of 11 one of her paintings was selected for display in the New York Metropolitan Museum of Art. She is supportive of many charities but in particular both the Lili Claire Foundation, a non-profit organisation to benefit those born with Williams syndrome and other neurogenetic defects, and the Rape Treatment Center at Santa Monica.

Sean Bean
'Boromir'

His real name was Shaun Mark Bean. Born in Sheffield on 17 April 1959, which may account for the fact that he is a devoted Sheffield United Football Club supporter and why perhaps he has a 100% Blade tattoo on his left shoulder.

His father, Brian, was a steel plater, with his own business, and his mother a secretary. He was educated at Brook Comprehensive and his obsession at school was football, playing inside right for the school team.

In 1975, aged 16, he left school, with two O levels, in Art and English and having decided that a career as a footballer was not for him, he was left undecided on his future. He sold cheese in a supermarket, shovelled snow in winter but then went to work for his father as a welder. His father sent him on day release for a welding course at Rotherham College of Arts and Technology, he came across an arts class and felt that his future was more in art than welding. He enrolled at Granville College but left immediately.

However, in September 1979, he started a Fine Arts foundation course at Rotherham College, but he came across a drama class and that was it. At college he played 'Arsenic And Old Lace', 'The Owl And The Pussycat' and also 'A Murder Has Been Arranged', as well as a number of Cabaret performances. Within six months he won a scholarship to RADA and he started there for his formal training in the spring of 1981.

At RADA he appeared first in 'Fear And Miseries Of The Third Reich' before turning to Shakespeare in King Lear, Twelfth Night and Julius Caesar. He was an outstanding student and won a silver medal for his performance as Pozzo in the graduation play, 'Waiting For Godot'.

After RADA he had a few small parts until, in 1985, he performed in 'Deathwatch' at The Young Vic, which led to various roles but in particular an invitation to join the Royal Shakespeare Company for their 1986/7 season. This was extended to early 1988, and he played at Stratford, London and Newcastle in performances of 'Romeo And Juliet', 'Fair Maid Of The West' and 'A Midsummer Night's Dream'.

He has been in a huge number of films including his part as Mellors, in 'Lady Chatterley's Lover', in 1992 and Trevelyan, Agent 006, in Goldeneye, in 1995. In 1993 he was cast as Richard Sharpe, the star of Bernard Cornwell's hit novels, and appeared on that series from 1993 to 1997. In 1997 he also took the part of Count Vronsky in 'Anna Karenina'. In 1999 he was seen playing the part of Andy McNab in Bravo Two Zero and the following year was in 'Essex Boys'.

However to date he may well be best remembered for his part, as Boromir, in 'The Lord Of The Rings' trilogy. In 2002, he returned to the stage after a 13-year absence to play Macbeth at the Albery Theatre.

He has been married three times, first to Debra James, in 1981, a hairdresser; secondly to Melanie Hill, an actress, in 1990, but they divorced in 1997, and with her he had two girls, Molly and Lorna. Thirdly he married, in 1997, Abigail Cruttenden, also an actress, with whom he had a girl Evie, but they too have divorced.

Jimmy Tarbuck OBE
'Busy Comedian'

The son of a bookmaker, he was born in Liverpool on 6 February 1940. He left school at 15 and started work as a garage mechanic but was sacked from that and many subsequent jobs for 'fooling around'. At 18, he joined a touring rock'n'roll show, starting him in showbusiness, before becoming a Butlin's holiday camp Redcoat.

At this time, at the age of 22, he was spotted by Val Parnell, and made his TV debut on 'Comedy Bandbox'. He then had several appearances on 'Sunday Night at the London Palladium' before becoming its regular compere, in 1965.

He was soon in the top variety shows throughout the country, made his London cabaret debut at The Talk of the Town and was appearing in the series, 'The Jimmy Tarbuck Show', 'It's Tarbuck' and 'Tarbuck's Luck'. He was also a regular in many Christmas pantomimes.

Between 1975 and 1986 he was appearing in his own television game show, 'Winner Takes All' and this was followed by 'Tarby's Frame Game', both for Yorkshire Television.

In the 1980s he signed a five-year contract with London Weekend Television to present 'Live from Her Majesty's', this was followed by 'Live from the Piccadilly' in 1986 and then by 'Live from the London Palladium'. He was also at the same time in the television series, 'Tarby and Friends'. All this was followed in 1988 by the series 'Tarby After Ten'.

He is regarded as one of England's leading after-dinner speakers and hosts many of the top award and business presentation shows as well as many TV guest appearances including, Parkinson, Dales's All Stars, The Clive James Show, The Mrs Merton Show, Call My Bluff, the Dale Winton Christmas Special and Celebrity Ready Steady Cook to name but a few.

His life is so busy it would be impossible to list all his appearances but the above is a brief smattering!

He has been awarded the top Variety Club of Great Britain award as Showbusiness Personality of the Year and in 1994 he was appointed OBE for his services to showbusiness and charity. He has also been made an Officer of the Most Venerable Order of the Hospital of St. John of Jerusalem. For his after dinner speaking he was awarded the 'Ivor Spencer Best After-Dinner Speaker Award for 1996' by the Guild of Professional Toastmasters.

He is very keen on golf, plays many charity golf matches, has been captain of Coombe Hill Golf Club, holds an annual 'The Jimmy Tarbuck Golf Classic' and made a comedy video 'Jimmy Tarbuck's Nightmare Holes of Golf'. He is also a life long supporter of Liverpool Football Club.

Married to Pauline they have two daughters, Lisa, the actress and presenter and Cheryl, an interior designer, and a son, James, who recently married Sacha, the only daughter of Toni and Pauline Mascolo, the founders of the Toni & Guy hairdressing empire.

David Jason OBE
'Del Boy'

Born David John White on 2 February 1940, in Edmonton; son of Arthur, a Billingsgate fish porter and Olwyn, his wife. He started his career as an electrician but at the same time was a keen amateur actor, before his actor brother, Arthur, helped him to get his first professional part in South Sea Bubble.

His TV career started in 1967 with the comedy 'Do Not Adjust Your Set', which was followed by his appearance in 'Counterstrike' in 1969, where he played Taffy Sadler and by 1974 he was playing along side Ronnie Barker in Porridge. In 1975 he was again working with Ronnie Barker in 'Open All Hours' where he played Granville, followed shortly thereafter by his performance as Shorty Mepstead in 'Lucky Feller'.

Perhaps he will always be best known for comic character Del Trotter in Only Fools and Horses, which was first shown in 1981 and has continued to amuse millions. The constant replay of the popular scene where Del Boy fails in his attempt to lean nonchalantly against the bar to produce the perfect fall will remind the public of his pleasure in carrying out his own stunts.

Not only is he a comedy actor but also plays straight and in 1987 he played the memorable Skullion, the Cambridge Porter, in Tom Sharpe's, 'Porterhouse Blue'. In 1992 he was playing the morose Inspector William 'Jack' Frost in the TV series 'A Touch of Frost' which has continued to be produced to much acclaim.

In 1989 he was playing Ted Simcock in 'A Bit of a Do', but perhaps the favourite character of all is his portrayal of the loveable Pop Larkin in 'The Darling Buds of May'. This series also brought Catherine Zeta-Jones to public attention and in many ways was the catalyst launching her subsequent career.

In 1993 he was in 'Bullion Boys' and appointed OBE. In 1998 he was March in 'March in Windy City' and the following year he was Frank Beck, a land agent at Sandringham, who creates a unit of Royal Servants who fight and suffer at Gallipoli, in 'All the King's Men'. He has also appeared as Wilkins Micawber in the TV drama series Micawber in 2001 and 'The Quest' in 2002.

His voice overs have included Wombling Free (1977); The Water Babies (1978); Danger Mouse (1981); The Wind in the Willows (1984); Count Duckula (1988) and The BFG (1989).

His awards include Best Actor Award, BAFTA,1988; Best Light Entertainment Performance Award, BAFTA, 1990; Special Recognition Award for Lifetime Achievement in Television, National Television Awards, 1996 and Best Comedy Performance Award, BAFTA, 1997.

Sadly, his partner of 18 years, Myfanwy Talog, died of cancer in 1995, but he now has a new partner, Gill Hinchcliffe, with whom he had a daughter, Sophie, in February 2001. When he is not in the limelight he pursues one of his great passions, diving, inspired having watched the Jacques Cousteau TV programmes as a lad. He also enjoys flying and motorcycles.

Sir Simon Rattle CBE
'Charismatic Conductor'

Appointed, in 2002, as the Chief Conductor and Artistic Adviser to the Berlin Philharmonic Orchestra, succeeding Claudio Abbado. He was born, in Liverpool, on 19 January 1955, to parents, who whilst musical enthusiasts were not professional musicians. He was, originally a percussionist and joined the Merseyside Youth Orchestra at the age of 11, moving on to the Royal Liverpool Orchestra at 15.

At 16, in 1971, he went on to the Royal Academy of Music, in London, and on 6 December 1973 he gave a performance of Mahler's Second Symphony, which first brought him to the attention of the professional world, and launched his conducting career. The following year, at Bournemouth, he became the youngest contestant ever to win the John Player International Conducting Competition. He then became the Assistant Conductor of both the Bournemouth Symphony and Sinfonietta, for three years. Subsequently working with the Royal Liverpool Philharmonic, BBC Scottish Symphony and Rotterdam Philharmonic, to name but as few.

In 1979, he made his North American debut with the Los Angeles Philharmonic Orchestra, and was its Principal Guest Conductor from 1981 until 1994. During this period he also conducted the Cleveland Orchestra and the Chicago, San Francisco, Toronto and Boston Symphony Orchestras.

In 1980 he took up the post of Principal Conductor and Artistic Adviser of the City of Birmingham Symphony Orchestra, and became its Music Director in 1990. He remained with it for a total of 18 years, and transformed it into a very successful and respected major orchestra. Known for his charismatic, innovative, dynamic style and his wide musical interests he has led, not only the North American Orchestras, but also the Vienna Philharmonic and, of course, the Glyndebourne Opera, where he made his debut in 1977 with the 'Cunning Little Vixen'. His debut at the Royal Opera House, in 1990, was also conducting that opera, whilst his debut with the National Opera was in 1985 with Katya Kabonova.

Since his debut, at Glyndebourne he has also conducted, Anadne auf Naxos, Der Rosenkavalier, Love for Three Oranges, Idomeneo, Porgy & Bess, Ravel's L'heure Espanole and L'enfant et les Sortileges. Also he has conducted there the Marriage of Figaro, Cosi fan Tutte and Don Giovanni.

In the 1987 New Years' Honours he was appointed CBE, for his services to music, and in the Birthday Honours list, in June 1994, he was knighted. He has received many other awards including, Officier des Arts et Lettres, in 1995; the Toepfer Foundation of Hamburg's 1996 Shakespeare Prize; the 1997 BBC Music Magazine Outstanding Achievement Award and in the same year, the RSA Albert Medal. He has also received the Outstanding Achievement award at the 1999 South Bank Show Awards.

An exclusive EMI artist, he has made over 60 recordings, many with the City of Birmingham Symphony Orchestra, and many of which have received prestigious international awards.

His first marriage, in 1980, to Elise Rose, an American soprano, with whom he had two sons, was dissolved in 1995. The following year he married Candice Allen but they separated in 2004.

Nic

Sir Elton John CBE
'Candle in the Wind'

He was born Reginald Kenneth Dwight on 25 March 1947, in Pinner, Middlesex to Stanley and Sheila Dwight. He was educated at Pinner County Grammar School before winning a scholarship, at the age of 11, and going on to the Royal Academy of Music, in London. His love of music began early in life, for at the age of four, he started taking piano lessons.

In 1961, at 14, he joined the local rhythm and blues band, Bluesology, and in 1965 turned professional joining them on a tour to the USA. Not particularly happy with the direction of the band's music he was fortunate, in 1967, to meet Bernie Turpin, an unknown writer from Lincolnshire with similar musical tastes. Their first composition was 'Scarecrow'.

In 1968 he and Bernie Taupin signed up as staff writers for Dick James's new company DJM. At that time, their songs made little impact. He also played piano in sessions with the Hollies and in particular on 'He Ain't Heavy He's My Brother'.

He made his break with his album 'Elton John', in 1970, which included the tracks 'Border Song' and 'Your Song', this was his first UK hit reaching number two in the charts. He then had further success that year with Tumbleweed Connection. Over the following years he achieved superstar status with concerts in the USA and was famous for his outrageous costumes and glasses. Between 1972 and 1975 he had seven consecutive number one albums. His various hit singles include, 'Rocket Man', 'Daniel', 'Goodbye Yellow Brick Road', 'Candle in the Wind' and 'Someone Saved My Life'.

In 1972 he changed his name by deed poll to Elton Hercules John, deriving the name Elton John from his former colleagues with Bluesology,

Elton Dean and Long John Baldry. The name Hercules was one of his songs from his 'Honky Chateau' album.

In 1976 his duet with Kiki Dee, 'Don't Go Breaking My Heart', reached the top of the UK charts and he released two further successful albums, 'Here And There' and 'Blue Moves'.

The 1980s proved to be not as successful as the previous decade although he did have some hits. He had a resurgence in 1992 with 'The One', which went double platinum. In 1994 he was inducted into the Rock 'n' Roll Hall of Fame and also collaborated with Tim Rice on the Lion King soundtrack for which he received an Oscar for Best Original Song for 'Can You Feel The Love Tonight', as well as a Grammy for Best Male Pop Performance. In 1997 he played a rewritten version of Candle In The Wind at the funeral of Princess Diana, this record for charity became the biggest selling record of all time. His work with Tim Rice has continued in the film 'El Dorado' and musical 'Aida'.

He was appointed CBE in 1995 and knighted, in 1998, for his contribution to music and fund raising for AIDS charities. In 1991 he established The Elton John AIDS Foundation and on its behalf he hosts an annual ball at his Windsor home, which is attended by the great, the good and the glamorous.

In 1984 he married the German sound engineer, Renate Blauel but the marriage only lasted a few months, they divorced in 1988. He has for many years been in a stable relationship with his partner, David Furnish, a filmmaker. He is a keen football supporter and rescued Watford Football Club becoming a director, chairman and now Life President.

Peter Gabriel
'Genesis'

He was born on 13 February 1950 to parents who have a great interest in music, Ralph and Irene and brought up in Chobham, Surrey.

He first made his name as the lead singer at Genesis, which had been started by him and a number of friends, whilst still at school, Charterhouse. In 1968 they released their first single, 'The Silent Sun' and the following year performed their first professional gig, at Brunel University.

He remained with Genesis for seven years, and during that time they produced the albums, 'From Genesis to Revelation', in 1969; 'Nursery Crime', in 1971; 'Foxtrot' came next which was released in October 1972. In July 1973 they released 'Genesis Live', which reached No 9 in the UK charts, then in October of that year they released 'Selling England by the Pound', followed in November 1974 by 'The Lamb Lies Down on Broadway'.

After a number of years of intense touring he announced his departure and left Genesis in 1975 in order to go solo. His first four solo albums were all called Peter Gabriel but were known as Car, Scratch, Melt and Security after their sleeves. I was released in 1977; II in 1978 and reached No 10 in the UK charts. III was released in 1980 and IV in 1982, they reached No 1 and No 4 respectively in the UK charts.

In 1983 he released 'Peter Gabriel Plays Live' which reached No 8 in the UK charts. His greatest success came in 1986 when he released 'So' which reached No 1 in the UK and No 2 in the USA and also that year he released the single 'Sledgehammer' which reached No 1 in the USA.

He has released a number of singles, too many to list but some of his albums are 'Shaking the Tree',

in 1990, 'Us', in 1992, which reached No 2 in the UK, 'Ovo', in 2000 and 'Up' in 2002. He was also commissioned to contribute music and act as musical director for the Millennium Dome show in London.

In 2000 he co-founded OD2, Online Distribution, which is the leading European platform provider for the distribution of online music.

His interest in music goes well beyond just recording, he was the Founder of WOMAD (World of Music, Arts and Dance) international festivals featuring traditional and modern music arts and dance aimed at encouraging new artists. He also founded 'Real World Group', in 1985; Real World Studios, in 1986; 'Real World Records', in 1989 and 'Real World Multimedia, in 1994. Real World has been focused on bridging the gap between high technology and multi-ethnic art.

Human rights have been of great interest to him and he was the joint founder of 'WITNESS', the human rights organisation which arms human rights activists with hand held video cameras, computers and means of communication so that they can record and help end human rights abuses. He released in August 1980 his anti-apartheid song 'Biko' which became one of the biggest protest anthems of the 1980s. It was named after Stephen Biko the murdered South African activist. He also became heavily involved with Amnesty International and recorded, with Senegalese star Youssou N'Dour. They toured the USA under the name of 'Conspiracy of Hope', raising funds for Amnesty.

In 1971 he married Jill Moore with whom he had two daughters. Following his divorce he married Meabh, in 2002 and they have a son.

Dame Stella Rimington DCB
'MI5, breaker of the glass ceiling'

The first lady Director General of MI5. She spent much of her career breaking the glass ceilings within that organisation. She joined MI5, in London, in 1969 when it was male dominated and chauvinistic. Over the years she changed all that.

Born to David Whitehouse, a mechanical engineer, and his wife, Muriel, in May 1935. She started life in South London but, at the age of four, because of the wartime dangers of living there, the family moved to Essex. However they were soon on their way to Barrow.

Although not a Roman Catholic, she attended the nun dominated Crosslands Convent School at Furness Abbey, but, at the age of 12, the family moved again, this time to the Midlands, where she attended Nottingham Girls' High School. It was while she was there that she met John, her husband to be, whilst travelling on the same school bus.

In October 1954 she went on to University at Edinburgh to read English. Uncertain of what to do next, she decided to go on a one-year diploma in the Study of Records and Administration of Archives. Her first employment followed when she became an Assistant Archivist at Worcester County Records Office. She had met up with John again when he was, up from Cambridge, visiting his parents who had moved there.

A decision to marry John meant a move to London, but John, a Civil Servant, was soon posted to the British High Commission, in New Delhi, as First Secretary (Economic). Not satisfied with her new role as a diplomat's wife she was recruited as a clerk/typist working for the MI5 representative at the High Commission. She admits that her typing was really only with two fingers.

With the posting to India ending in 1969, they returned to England and she took up a post at MI5 as an Assistant Officer, initially spending her time checking out the UK members of the Communist Party, before soon moving on to the newly formed Irish Section.

Breaking the glass ceiling, in 1973, to become an Officer prior to leaving the service to follow John, once again, this time on his two year posting to Brussels. She returned in 1976 and rejoined MI5 holding various posts in the Agents section until being promoted, in 1983, to Assistant Director of a section in the counter-subversion branch. Her time there spanned a period of considerable political upheaval, the miners' strike, Greenham Common protests, the height of CND, the growth of Militant Tendency and its activities in Liverpool and the Socialist Workers Party becoming very active in the Universities.

By December 1986 she had become Director of Counter-espionage, known as K, after the founder of MI5, Brigadier Vernon Kell. She was the first woman ever to reach this level in MI5. She became Director General in 1992, not only the first female but was also the first to be publicly named, which helped to bring more openness to MI5 but the publicity which came with that increased the stress to her and her daughters. She has also written her autobiography, Open Secret, and a novel, At Risk.

Retiring from MI5 in 1996 she was created a Dame Commander of the Bath. She joined the boards of Marks & Spencer plc, Whitehead Mann GKR and British Gas plc. She has two daughters, Sophie and Harriet but whilst she has remained married to John they are separated and have for many years lived very separate lives.

The Hon. Sir Jonathon Porritt CBE
'Protector of the Environment'

He was born on 6 July 1950 in London, the son of Baron Porritt GCMG, GCVO, OBE and his wife Kathleen. He was educated at Eton before going on to Magdalen College, Oxford from where he graduated with a First Class degree in Modern Languages.

At the age of 25, he abandoned training as a barrister, to become an English teacher with the Inner London Education Authority. In 1980 he was appointed Head of English and Drama at Burlington Danes School, London.

While still teaching, in 1977, he stood as a candidate for the Ecology Party in the local government elections and, in 1979, he stood at the general election and for the European Parliament. He served as Chairman of the Ecology Party, now known as the Green Party, from 1979 to 1980 and again from 1982 to 1984. He then stood again as a candidate in the 1983 general election and the 1984 European elections.

In 1984 he gave up teaching to become a director of Friends of the Earth and under his leadership its numbers of supporters rose from 12,700 to 226,300. He stayed running Friends of the Earth until 1996 when he left to set up a charity called Forum for the Future. Its aims are to persuade businesses to improve their environmental performance and has advised many of the major UK companies, including Tescos and ICI.

His dedication to the protection of the environment and to charity led the Prime Minister to appointing him chairman, in 2000, of the then recently formed Sustainable Development Commission. Its job is to promote sustainable development across all sectors of the UK and in particular its tasks include, identifying key unsustainable trends, encouraging and stimulating good practice and acting as a 'critical friend' to the government in appraising its performance in delivering sustainable development.

In addition, he is a member of the Board of the South West Regional Development Agency, a trustee of the World Wildlife Fund for Nature and a Vice-President of the Socialist Environment Resources Association.

He has had many publications including, 'Seeing Green – the Politics of Ecology', in 1984, 'Friends of the Earth Handbook', in 1987, 'The Coming of the Greens' in 1988, 'Where on Earth are we Going', in 1991 and in the same year, 'Captain Eco', which was written for children. In 1990 he presented, for the BBC TV, the programme 'Where on earth are we going?'.

In the Millennium Honours list he was appointed CBE for his services to environmental protection and, in 2003 he was awarded an honorary Doctorate of Law (HonLLD) by the University of Greenwich.

He married Sarah Staniforth in 1986 and they, and their two daughters, live in Cheltenham.

Professor Lord Robert Winston
'Fertility Expert'

He was born on 15 July 1940, the son of Laurence and Ruth Winston and was educated at St Paul's School, London, before going on to London University to study medicine. Following qualification in 1964 he held a number of junior posts at the London Hospital.

In 1970 he joined the Hammersmith Hospital as a Registrar and became involved in research and development of gynaecological microsurgery. He was the scientific adviser to the World Health Organisation on contraceptive matters and reproductive research from 1975 until 1980 and carried out the first human tubal transplant in 1976. He also founded the NHS's in-vitro fertilisation programme in 1981.

He has written over 300 scientific publications for magazines such as Science, Nature and The Lancet and is a regular contributor to the papers. He has also written a number of books including, 'Human Instinct', 'Infertility', 'Getting Pregnant, 'Making Babies', 'Genetic Manipulation' and 'The IVF Revolution'.

He has also presented popular television science series; 'Your Life in Their Hands', 'The Human Body', which received three BAFTAs and a Peabody award, 'Making Babies', 'Secret Life of Twins', 'The Superhuman', which received the Wellcome Award for Medicine and Biology, 'Child of our Time' and 'Human Instinct'.

He was created a life peer, Lord Winston of Hammersmith, in 1995, taking the Labour Party whip. He regularly speaks in the House of Lords on education, science, medicine and the arts and is a member of the select committee on science and technology and Chairman of the All-party Parliamentary Group on Reproductive Health.

He ran an appeal for Queen Charlotte's raising over £13 million to build and equip the most advanced reproductive research centre in Europe, with space for 130 scientists and doctors working to improve the health of women and babies.

Since 1990 his team at the Hammersmith Hospital has established many improvements in fertility medicine and IVF treatment including the birth of the first baby after DNA tests to avoid sex-linked disease, such as muscular dystrophy and haemophilia and the identification of embryonic single gene defects, such as cystic fibrosis. Further achievements include the birth of the first baby after embryonic chromosome screening, the birth of the first baby after total body irradiation for maternal leukaemia and the first pregnancy after screening embryos for chromosome translocations.

He has received numerous awards for his work including a Wellcome Senior Research Fellowship, 1973 to 1977, a Blair-Bell Lectureship RCOG, in 1978, the Cedric Carter Medal, Clinical Genetics Society, in 1993 and an Honorary Fellowship from Queen Mary and Westfield College. He was also Gold Medallist for the Royal Society of Health, in 1998, received the BMA Gold Award for Medicine in the Media, in 1999 and, in the same year, the Faraday Gold Medal from The Royal Society.

In 1973 he married Lira Feigenbaum and they have two sons and a daughter. His interests include music, wine, broadcasting and the theatre, he directed an award-winning production of 'Each in his Own Way' at the Edinburgh Festival in 1969.

John Simpson CBE
'Intrepid War Correspondent'

He was born on 9 August 1944 and was brought up in London and Suffolk by his father, Roy, following his parents' separation. He was educated at St Paul's School, in London before he went on to Magdalene College, Cambridge where he read English. Whilst at Cambridge he edited the Granta, the magazine at that time published for and by the students of Cambridge University.

In 1966 he joined the BBC as a trainee sub-editor in the Radio Newsroom. He became a reporter for BBC Radio News in 1970 was well known early in his career when Harold Wilson, the then Prime Minister, punched him in the stomach for asking whether Mr Wilson was about to call a general election.

He has been with the BBC for over 30 years and became the Dublin correspondent, in 1972 before becoming the Common Market correspondent, based in Brussels in 1975. In 1977 he moved to Johannesburg to become the South Africa correspondent and the following year became the Diplomatic correspondent for BBC Television News and in 1980 became the BBC Political Editor.

1981 saw him as Presenter and Correspondent, BBC TV News and from 1982 to 1988 he was Diplomatic Editor for BBC TV. We know him best today as the BBC's World Affairs Editor where he has reported from more than 100 countries, from 30 war zones and interviewed numerous world leaders from Margaret Thatcher to Colonel Gadhaffi.

In 1991 he was the BBC's key correspondent in Baghdad during the Gulf War and, despite being ordered to leave by his employers, he stayed on in the City. He has covered many of the major upheavals throughout the world and in

Romania on the night of Ceaucescu's execution he used Ceaucescu's own pen, which the housekeeper had given him earlier in the day, to write Ceaucescu's obituary.

He was the associate editor of The Spectator between 1990 and 1996 and since then has written a foreign affairs column for The Sunday Telegraph. He has also written many books including 'Behind Iranian Lines', in 1988; 'Despatches from the Barricades', in 1990; 'From the House of War': covering Baghdad and the Gulf, in 1991; 'The Darkness Crumbles': the death of Communism, in 1992; 'In the Forests of the Night': drug running and terrorism in Peru, in 1993 and his autobiographical trilogy, 'Strange Places, Questionable People', in 1998; 'A Mad World, My Masters', in 2000 and 'News from No Man's Land', in 2002.

He was appointed CBE in the Gulf War Honours of 1991 and has twice been named the Royal Television Society's Journalist of the Year, 1991 and 2000. He has received a number of other awards including three BAFTAs, a Golden Nymph award for his reporting of Ayatollah Khomeini's return to Iran in 1979, a Peabody Trust award for news in 1999, a special jury's award at the Bayeux War Correspondents Awards in 2002 and an International Emmy award for News Coverage for his report, for the BBC Ten O'Clock News, on the fall of Kabul. In September 1999 his old Cambridge College awarded him an honorary fellowship and, in 2003, he received an Honorary degree of LLD from the University of Dundee in recognition of his unique contributions to broadcasting.

In 1965 he married Diane Petteys, with whom he had two daughters. Following his divorce in 1995, he married Adèle Krüger.

John Humphrys
'The Today Programme'

Born in Splott, Cardiff, on 17 August 1943, he was educated at Cardiff High School but left at the age of 15 to work, first for the Penarth Times before moving on to the Western Mail. When working there he changed the spelling of his surname from Humphries to avoid confusion with a namesake working with him on that paper.

He next moved into television with the Cardiff-based commercial station TWW until, in 1966, he moved to join the BBC, based in Liverpool. The following year he became the northern industrial correspondent and was also covering Northern Ireland. By the age of 28 he had become the corporation's first full-time TV correspondent in the USA and spent six years there, covering stories in both North and South America including the Watergate affair and resignation of President Nixon on the one hand and the revolution in Chile on the other.

In 1977, he was sent to South Africa, where amongst other things, he covered the transfer of power in Zimbabwe. He returned to England, three years later, for a year as a diplomatic correspondent. In September 1981 he became one of the main BBC News presenters, presenting the Nine O'clock News. He moved on, in 1987, to host Radio 4's Today Programme, at which he has continued ever since.

In June 2003 the BBC chose him to host a new series of Mastermind, replacing the previous host, Magnus Magnusson. He has also hosted the BBC Sunday programme, 'On the Record' and similarly the Radio 4 programme, 'On the Ropes'. He continues to be a very popular after dinner speaker.

He has received honorary degrees from a number of Universities, including LLDs from Warwick, in 2003 and St Andrews, in 1999. His other awards include, Journalist of the Year, in 2000, the Variety Club Radio Personality of the Year, in 2001, a silver platter for Crystal Clear Broadcasting from the Plain English Campaign and, in 2003, the Gold Sony Radio Award.

Renowned for his combative interviewing style, there are Cabinet Ministers who try to avoid being interviewed by him and even following the Hutton Report the chances of a Cabinet Minister being given an easy time by him are slim. He has been quoted as saying; "taking on a Cabinet Minister is nothing to handling a kicking cow", he should know as he has spent tens years as an organic dairy farmer in his spare time. When, in 1995, Jonathon Aitken accused him of "poisoning the well of democratic debate", it triggered huge pro-Humphry support among both listeners and media; even the Daily Mail, which described him as 'one of the most brilliant journalists in the country'.

He was first married to Edna Wilding, in 1965 with whom he had a son and a daughter but they were divorced in 1991. In 2000, he had a son with his current partner, Valerie Sanderson. He also has a younger brother, Bob, who is also on television as the sports correspondent for BBC Wales.

Nic

Alistair Cooke KBE
'Letter from America'

Born, Alfred Cooke, in Salford on 20 November 1908, the son of an iron-fitter who was also a Methodist lay preacher. He was raised in Blackpool, in his parents' guesthouse, where he first came into contact with Americans on their way to the Front during World War 1.

He was educated at Blackpool Grammar School before being granted a scholarship to Cambridge where he obtained a First Class Honours Degree in English Literature. In 1932 he travelled to America on a Commonwealth Fund Fellowship attending Yale and Harvard.

He joined the BBC in 1934 as a film critic and in the same year married his first wife, Ruth Emerson with whom he had a son, Johnny, in 1940. In 1937 he emigrated to America and became a US citizen in 1941. He served as foreign correspondent for The Times and was the chief US correspondent for the Guardian for 24 years.

In March 1946 he started his 13 minute, world renowned Letter from America. The run was supposed to last for just three months, but he says 'they forgot' and it lasted 58 years with 2869 programmes having missed only 3 and broadcasting 16 from his hospital bed. He sent his last Letter from America in March 2004 retiring from his show; the world's longest running speech radio programme. His death occurred very shortly thereafter on 30 March 2004.

In an interview in 1987 he explained his technique "I sit down about 11 in the morning and then type, Good Evening and...then quite honestly I say, Now What?" "This is not being glib about it – I used to make notes all through the week about what I felt it would be responsible to talk about, but then I realised after several years that when you go to a dinner party or have a drink with a friend, you don't walk in with little cards, there have been presidents who have done that..." "I prefer to trust on my unconscious, automatic memory or whatever, and think of something that happened, of course, if a president is about to abdicate, you're going to talk about that, but most of the time I simply do not know when I sit down and it comes out. It takes about two hours then I come down to the BBC and do it."

In 1969, the then incoming Radio 4 controller, Tony Whitby, told colleagues he was determined to boot Cooke off the air, but Cooke, noted for friends in high places, simply rang the Chairman, and as Cliff Michelmore is reported as saying 'that was that.' He never joined the staff of the BBC, always remaining freelance, and when again it was suggested that he had passed his sell-by date the higher echelons of the BBC took the decision to support him so that he could 'die at the microphone'.

He felt he had a mission to explain the American way of thinking to the people of the UK and vice versa; a bridge across the pond. In the early 1970s his 13 hour television series, America: A Personal History was broadcast on both sides of the Atlantic earning him an honorary knighthood (KBE).

In 1946 he married his second wife, Jane, a portrait painter, who bore him a daughter, Susie, born in 1949. Much of their married life has been spent between their Manhattan apartment, over looking Central Park and their cliff-top home on Long Island. He is well respected, so much so that he was asked to address the United States Congress on its 200th Anniversary and in 1991 he received a special award for his contribution to Anglo-American relations.

Henry Blofeld OBE
'My dear old thing'

The quintessential voice of Test Match Special has the ability to 'prattle' on, especially when the inclement English weather permits only a few pigeons on the cricket square and the odd plane or double-decker bus in view.

He was born on 23 September 1939 to a wealthy landowning Norfolk family that had acquired, through marriage, the Hoveton estate in the middle of the seventeenth century. His elder brother, Sir John Blofeld QC DL, a barrister, became a High Court Judge and took on the estate.

In 1947 he was sent to boarding school, Sunningdale prep school, where he was introduced to cricket and where he soon was chosen to represent the school. It was here that, following a shoulder injury, he donned his first set of wicket keeping gloves, which firmly established him in that position.

Then, on to Eton, where he became Captain of Cricket, with a great cricketing future ahead of him. However, in his final term, when bicycling to nets to pick the side for the following Saturday's match against Marlborough, he was severely injured when he collided with a coach carrying a gaggle of French members of the Women's Institute.

He recovered sufficiently quickly to be able to return for an inter house match, but really he never quite recovered from the accident. During his convalescence he had missed the entrance exams to King's College, Cambridge but the powers that be decided to admit him anyway.

On to Cambridge, where he received a blue for cricket, and clearly spent more time in the nets and on the square than at his studies. He dropped out before attaining his degree to pursue a career in merchant banking. Luckily, for the cricket fan and radio listener, this did not last and he turned his attention to his true love, cricket.

He joined Test Match Special in the 1970s and from then until the present day he has devoted his life to cricket. He left TMS for a short spell with BskyB but returned to Radio 4 in 1994. He also had a spell away in 2000 having heart surgery but managed to write his autobiography, 'A Thirst For Life'. He has also written a number of cricketing books and has, of course, written for all the major broadsheets.

From his world wide cricketing travels he has a wealth of stories and is an amusing speaker. He recalls his first time commentating at Old Trafford; 'it was raining; Johnners had been speaking for twenty minutes, when he, Blowers, entered the commentary box to take over. He then spoke eloquently for seven and three quarter minutes before turning round to find the box empty but for a note saying, "Keep going to 6.30pm and remember to handover to the studio". It was 2.30pm. Fortunately Johnners returned a few minutes later'.

He was appointed OBE in 2003, which to his amusement was described by one of his radio colleagues as standing for 'Odd But Entertaining'. Twice married; first to Joanna Hebeler, in April 1961, with whom he had a daughter Suki, who was born in September 1963; and secondly to Bitten Perert-Hanson, in October 1990.

How to Order

Further copies of this title can be obtained from:
People of the Day Limited
Sunnymede
New England Hill
West End
Woking
Surrey GU24 9PY

Telephone: 01276 858037
Facsimile: 01276 859483
web site: www.peopleoftheday.net

Payment can either be made by credit card (Visa only accepted) or by sending a cheque or postal order made payable to **People of the Day Ltd.**
DO NOT SEND CASH OR CURRENCY

Please add the following to cover postage and packing:
UK: £1.50 for the first book, and 50p for each additional book.
Overseas and Eire: £2.50 for the first book, and £1.00 for each additional book.

BLOCK CAPITALS PLEASE

Address of Cardholder:

Postcode

Delivery Address (if different from Cardholder):

Postcode

☐ I enclose my remittance for £ _____   ☐ Please debit my VISA card

Card Number

Expiry Date   Last 3 digits on signature strip

Signature

Prices and availability are subject to change without notice.

How to Order

Further copies of this title can be obtained from:
People of the Day Limited
Sunnymede
New England Hill
West End
Woking
Surrey GU24 9PY

Telephone: 01276 858037
Facsimile: 01276 859483
web site: www.peopleoftheday.net

Payment can either be made by credit card (Visa only accepted) or by sending a cheque or postal order made payable to **People of the Day Ltd.** **DO NOT SEND CASH OR CURRENCY**

Please add the following to cover postage and packing:
UK: £1.50 for the first book, and 50p for each additional book.
Overseas and Eire: £2.50 for the first book, and £1.00 for each additional book.

BLOCK CAPITALS PLEASE

Address of Cardholder:

_____

_____

_____

Postcode _____

Delivery Address (if different from Cardholder): _____

_____

_____

Postcode _____

☐ I enclose my remittance for £ _____   ☐ Please debit my VISA card

Card Number

☐☐☐☐ ☐☐☐☐ ☐☐☐☐ ☐☐☐☐

Expiry Date   Last 3 digits on signature strip

☐☐☐☐   ☐☐☐

Signature

Prices and availability are subject to change without notice.